Study Blast

Facts

CompTIA

Server+

SK0-003

by Matt Satori
2013-2014

CompTIA® Server+ Certification Study Guide

SK0-003

By Matt Satori

First Edition

© Study Blast Books

Http:\\www.studyblastbooks.com

U.S.

Table of Content

Certified Server+ Technician Exam

The CompTIA Server+ certification exam covers system hardware, software, storage, best practices in an IT environment, disaster recovery and troubleshooting.

Get your blast of knowledge. Study Blast gives you items you need to learn to pass your test!!

What is a Study Blast?

A "Study Blast" is a book of facts and items listed out for you to read, learn and memorize before taking a test. What can you do with the book? Try making flashcards from the items that give you difficulty. Read through before taking a practice test. Review after your practice tests. Read this book the night before the exam. Make your own quizzes and tests. Use this book for group studies. All that and more...

We review all the latest data and present it here. And by all means we are not a replacement for the "Official Study Guide" but we are an add on for every test taker to benefit from in helping them pass an exam.

Exam Information

CompTIA Network+ Examination

Exam Info:

From CompTIA.org

Number of questions	100
Length of test	90 minutes

Passing score	750 (on a scale of 100-900)
Recommended Experience	CompTIA A+ certification
Languages	English, Chinese, German, Japanese
Exam Code	SK0-003

To Register please go first to Http://www.compTIA.org

Notice

Knowledge and best practice in this field are constantly changing. As new research and experience broaden our knowledge, changes in practice, treatment and drug therapy may become necessary or appropriate. Readers are advised to check the most current information provided (i) on procedures featured or (ii) by the manufacturer of each product to be administered, to verify the recommended items, the method and duration of administration, and contraindications. To the fullest extent of the law, neither the Publisher nor the Editors assumes any liability for any injury and/or damage to persons or property arising out or related to any use of the material contained in this book.

Server Plus

Server Review

types of servers housing
rack-mounts

pedestals

how much is one U

1.75

pedestal design
similar in appearance to an extra0wide full-tower desktop case.

Used in smaller netwroks because they tend to be less expensive

PCI
Peripheral Componente Interconnect

multi-tier servers are subdivided
front-end

mid-tier

back-end

appliance server
provide a single service

distributed application
email

peer-to-peer application
sharing of computer goods and services

proxy server is capable of two types of cache requests
reverser proxy cache

forward proxy cache

Reverse proxy cache

cache is configured to act as the original server from which the client requests the data

Forward proxy cache

the client requests the Internet data and this requests is forwarded through the cache on the way to the original server

bce attack

the hacker misuses the PORT cmd on a FTP server to indirectly access arbitrary ports on other machines, or systems, not directly accessible by other means. When the hacker is connected, he or she is free to bypass any access controls that would otherwise apply

hammering

the repeated attempt to connect with an unavailable FTP server without permitting a normal delay time between attempts, FTP servers cannot process an unlimited numbers of requests, and when running at full capacity, they deny further access until capacity is freed, Causes server

FXP vulnerability

A FTP client connects to two servers at the same time, with one server directed to receive an incoming file, and the other instructed to send it. The sending and receiving servers connect to each other, and transfer the requested file without it first being copied to the originating FTP client. This can cause damage. FXP needs to be disabled

SNA server

allows client to access mainframe and mid-range data facilities, and also permits print facilities to be located on the host computer

HIS
Host Integration Service

succeeded SNA Server

allows seamless mainframe-to-desktop file transfer

height of a full rack
42u = 73.5 inches

nlb

ha

erp
network load balancing

high availability

enterprise resource planning

crm

oltp

mns
content relationship management

on-line transaction processing

majority node set

MNS

majority node set

stores the quorum on locally attached storage device, with one connected directly to each of the cluster nodes. Requires at least 3 nodes and more than the half need to be present

up to how many nodes NLV support

32 nodes

SMP

symmetrical multiprocessing parallel

lmic

locally managed internet connections

computer racks

19" wide (sometimes 23" wide)

2 mounting rails 0.625" each

31.5" or 39.4" deep

1-10-100 rule

feel 1mA of current through your body

10mA - makes your muscles contract to the point where you can't let go of a power source

100mA - sufficient to stop your heart

Common voltages provided by PS
+3.3

-5

+5

+12

VRM
Voltage regulator module

provides the appropriate supply voltage to the processor

Molex connector

Berg connector
old cd connectors

small floppy drives

Yellow cable voltage

Red cable voltage

Black cable voltage
Yellow - +12v

Red - +5v

Black - Ground

20-pin ATX

Orange - 1,2,11 - +3.3v

Red - 4,6,19,20 - +5v

Black - 3,5,7,13,15,16,17 - Ground

Gray - 8 - +5v

Purple - 9 - +5v

Yellow - 10 - +12v

Blue - 12 - -12v

Green - 14 - +5v

White - 18 - -5v

24-pin ATX
Orange - 1,2,12 - +3.3v

Red - 4,6,21,22,23 - +5v

Black - 3,5,7,15,17,18,19,24 - Ground

Gray - 8 - Power-Good signal

Purple - 9 - +5v

Yellow - 10,11 - +12v

Blue - 14 - -12v

Brown - 13 - +3.3v

Green - 16 - PS_ON# should be +5v

No color - 20 - Reserved

smt
simultaneous multi-threading technology

Allows OS to handle multi core processor

pipelining
the overlapping of the steps involved in processing instructions. Instructions are normally fetched, decoded, and executed, and result is written out to memory. This steps get overlapped to speed up execution. While one instruction is being executed, another is being decoded, and a third is being fetched.

register renaming
a technique by which modern processors can rename registers so that instructions can access their own set of registers and not interfere with other instructions. When multiple instructions are running at the same time, there's a chance that two will attempt to read pr write to the same register simultaneously

superpipelining
an improvement over pipelining. Super pipelining uses a larger number of shorter stages and support for a higher clock rate to improve performance

24-pin ATX
Orange - 1,2,12 - +3.3v

Red - 4,6,21,22,23 - +5v

Black - 3,5,7,15,17,18,19,24 - Ground

Gray - 8 - Power-Good signal

Purple - 9 - +5v

Yellow - 10,11 - +12v

Blue - 14 - -12v

Brown - 13 - +3.3v

Green - 16 - PS_ON# should be +5v

No color - 20 - Reserved

smt
simultaneous multi-threading technology

Allows OS to handle multi core processor

pipelining
the overlapping of the steps involved in processing instructions. Instructions are normally fetched, decoded, and executed, and result is written out to memory. This steps get overlapped to speed up execution. While one instruction is being executed, another is being decoded, and a third is being fetched.

register renaming
a technique by which modern processors can rename registers so that instructions can access their own set of registers and not interfere with other instructions. When multiple instructions are running at the same time, there's a chance that two will attempt to read pr write to the same register simultaneously

superpipelining

an improvement over pipelining. Superpipelining uses a larger number of shorter stages and support for a higher clock rate to improve performance

superscalar

a technique that enables a processor to execute more than one instruction in a single clock cycle

throttling

a technique by which the speed of the processor is scaled back so that it uses less power and creates less heat. Throttling reduces performance. It's most useful with portable computers, for which low power consumption and low heat production are critical design factors.

PDIP

Plastic dual inline package

8080, 8086, 8088

PGA

Pin grid array

80286, 80386, 80486, Xeon

CPGA

Ceramic pin grid array

AMD Socket A and Duron

SPGA

Staggered pin grid array

Pentium, Pentium MMX, Pentium Pro

PPGA
Plastic pin grid array

Pentium Pro, Celeron, Pentium III

FC-PGA
Flip chip pin grid array

P3, P4 and Celeron

OPGA
Organic ping grid array

AMD Athlon XP

SECC
Single Edge Contact Cartrdige

P2, P2 Xeon, P3 Xeon

SEP
Single edge process

Celeron

FCBGA
Flip chip ball grid array

Xeon

LGA
Land grid array

Celeron D, P4, P4 D, Core2 Duo

SLOT A

Socket A
AMD Athlon

AMD Athlon and Duron

Socket 5

Socket 7
Pentium

AMD K5 and K6,Cyrix

Socket 8

Socket 423
Pentium Pro

Pentium 4

Socket 478

Socket 370
Celeron, P4, P D

Celeron, Celeron II, P 3

Slot 1

Slot 2

LGA775
P2, Celeron, P3

P2 and Xeon

Celeron, P4, P D, Core2 Duo

A server was recently installed with all necessary hardware and software.

Before placing the server into service, a(n)_____should be created.
performance baseline

A UPS is being selected for a remote office. The correct size UPS needs to be

determined.

Which formula should be used to determine the load requirements?
Watts = Current x Voltage

Explanation: Power [Watts] = Current x Volts

1.SCSI

2.Wide SCSI

3.Fast SCSI

4.Fast Wide SCSI

5.Ultra SCSI

6.Wide Ultra SCSI

7.Ultra2 SCSI

8.Wide Ultra2 SCSI

9.Ultra3 SCSI
1.SCSI - 5MB @ 8bits

2.Wide SCSI - 10MB @ 16bits

3.Fast SCSI - 10MB @ 8bits

4.Fast Wide SCSI - 20MB @ 16bits

5.Ultra SCSI - 20MB @ 8bits

6.Wide Ultra SCSI - 40MB @ 16bits

7.Ultra2 SCSI - 40MB @ 8bits

8.Wide Ultra2 SCSI - 80MB @ 16bits

9.Ultra3 SCSI - 160MB @ 16bits

SCSI Signaling?

The 3 type of SCSI signaling

SCSI Signaling - The manner that a SCSI interface sends signal down the cable.

3 Types - Single End, High Voltage Difference & Low Voltage Difference

CISC
Complex Instruction Set Computing.

bios shadowing
at startup the BIOS is copied in the regular memory.

CMOS
complementary metal oxide semiconductor

EPP

ECP
Enhanced Parallel Port

Extended Capabilities Parallel Port

APM

ACPI
Advanced Power Management

Advanced Configuration and Power Interface

CMOS contains the
BIOS

List volatile memory

RAM

CMOS

List non-volatile memory

ROM

PROM

EPROM

EEPROM

Flash

ROM

PROM

EPROM

EEPROM

ROM - read only memory

PROM - programmable read only memory

EPROM - erasable programmable read only memory

EEPROM - electronically erasable programmable read only memory

Main dif. between DRAM and SRAM

DRAM - requires the memory to be refreshed 100 times per sec to keep its content

SRAM - doesn't need to be refreshed it's simpler

DRAM is smaller and cheaper than SRAM

SRAM mainly for L2 and L3 caches

DRAM - memory access
CPU sends the row address and then sends the column address to access a cell

Speed of the RAM Connection
Directly controls how fast the computer can access instructions and data, and therefore has a big effect on system performance.

FPM - memory access
Fast Page Mode - CPU sends a row address, followed by a column address. If the CPU needs more cells from the same row, it can send just the column address

Dual Data Rate (DDR) Memory
The memory can transmit data twice per cycle instead of once, which makes the memory faster.

VRAM - memory access
Video DRAM - modified version of FPM. One port can read to refresh the image on screen, while the other can be used to generate the next image to be displayed

EDO - memory access
Extended Data Out - Works like FPM, except that a new cell access request can begin before a previous request has finished

BEDO - memory access
Burst Extended Data Out - Add pipelining tech to EDO to improve performance

ADRAM - memory access

Asynchronous DRAM - Is synchronized with the system clock. Regardless of the clock's speed, ADRAM takes the same amount of time to access and return data from a memory cell

SDRAM - memory access
Synchronous DRAM - sync with the system's clock to improve performance. Internal interleaving enables overlapped access ad EDO

DRDRAM - memory access
Direct Rambus DRAM - Uses a 16-bit data bus running at up to 800MHz, transferring data on both the rise and fall of the clock signal

DDR - memory access
Double Data Rate - doubles the transfer rate by transferring data on both the rise and fall of the clock signal. DDR memory module transfer data on a bus that is 64 data bits wide

DDR transfer rate

DDR2 transfer rate

DDR3 transfer rate
DDR transfer rate - 200-400 Mhz

DDR2 transfer rate - 400-1066 Mhz

DDR3 transfer rate - 800-1600 Mhz

what's SNMP's main security weakness
it transfers data in clear text ASCII

what are 3 added features in SNMPv2

1)New trap format 2)Trap transfer from one NMS to another 3)Partial bulk data transfer

what are snmp server management consoles often called

enterprise management consoles

what is the name of the blade server enclosure

blade center

What is the clock, bus width and transfer rate of Ultra2 SCSI?

40Mhz, 8bit, 40MB/s

Fibre Channel distance limits (copper/fiber)

Copper: 30 meters

Fiber: 10 kilometers

What environments are blade servers suited to

Tier1 and tier2 environments such as email, web, directory, firewalls, etc

Number of devices with Ultra SCSI?

8

What is the clock, bus width and transfer rate of Fast-Wide SCSI?

10Mhz, 8bit, 20MB/s

How many devices can you have on a SCSI-3 RAID 5 controller?

Dual Channel?
15

30

hba

NMS

DMI

MIB
host bus adapter

network management system

Desktop Management Interface

SNMP Database

Appliances servers
provide a single or multiple server

At what 2 voltages do universal 32-bit PCI cards run at?
3.3v and 5v

What are 2 added features in SNMPv3?
Added security

remote configuration

What is the clock, bus width and transfer rate of Ultra SCSI?
20Mhz, 8bit, 20MB/s

What is the clock, bus width and transfer rate of Ultra3 SCSI?
40*2Mhz, 8bit, 80MB/s

Three server form factors
Pedestal, rack mountable and blade

Number of devices with Ultra SCSI?
16

CPU Expansion Bus speed
the speed the PCI bus can run at

How can you tell the MB through put of a PCI bus
Bytes x clock cycle

CPU Expansion bus speed describes what?
PCI bus speed

What are the 3 basic components in the SNMP model?
Managed Devices

Agents

Network Management System NMS

What do you call a PCI card that can be Hot Swapped?
Hot-Plug PCI

What is the clock, bus width and transfer rate of Fast SCSI?
10Mhz, 8bit, 10MB/s

What is the clock, bus width and transfer rate of Ultra Wide SCSI?
20Mhz, 16bit, 40MB/s

What port do SNMP Traps use?
162

Fibre Channel: # of drives
126

What is the clock, bus width and transfer rate of Ultra2 Wide SCSI?
40*2Mhz, 16bit, 80MB/s

What port do SNMP Events use?
161

How many U's is a typical blade server?
3U's

Common Channel Protocols
HPPI and SCSI

What RAID system protects against 2 drives failing at the same time?

RAID 1+0

What is the clock, bus width and transfer rate of SCSI-1?

5Mhz, 8bit, 5MB/s

What is the clock, bus width and transfer rate of Ultra3 Wide SCSI?

40*2Mhz, 16bit, 160MB/s

What's the major difference between a SAN and a NAS

The data addressing scheme

How many U's are in a rack?

42U's

ACR

advance communication riser

backward compatible with AMR

AMR

Audio/Modem Riser

used to provide both audio and video support

CNR

communication and networking riser

provides modem, audio and LAN interface

IRQ 0

IRQ 1

IRQ 2

IRQ 3

IRQ 4

IRQ 5
IRQ 0 - System time

IRQ 1 - keyboard

IRQ 2 - cascade 9 - 15

IRQ 3 - COM2

IRQ 4 - COM1

IRQ 5 - Sound or LPT2

IRQ 6

IRQ 7

IRQ 8

IRQ 9

IRQ 10

IRQ 11
IRQ 6 - FDD

IRQ 7 - LPT1

IRQ 8 - Real-time clock

IRQ 9 - Various

IRQ 10 - Various

IRQ 11 - Various

IRQ 12

IRQ 13

IRQ 14

IRQ 15
IRQ 12 - ps/2 mouse

IRQ 13 - FPU

IRQ 14 - Primary IDE

IRQ 15 - Secondary IDE

DMA

PCI

ISA
direct memory access

peripheral component interconnect

industry standard architecture

PC/XT bus
width - 8 bit

clock speed - 4.77 MHz

data rate - 1.6MBps

PC/AT aka ISA
width - 16 bit

clock speed - 8 MHz

data rate - 8MBps

PCI
width - 32/64 bit

clock speed - 33/66 MHz

data rate - 133/533 MBps

PCIx
width - 64bit

data rate - 1064 MBps

Parallel required additional logic to synch data signals.

If combined with a slower device runs at the slower speed

PCIe
full duplex, serial

supported

widths x1,x2,x4,x8,x16,x32

PCIe link
connection between a PCIe device and the system

PCIe lane
each lane uses a dedicated, bidirectional, serial, point-to-point connection called lane

UDMA

ADHI
ultra DMA

Advanced Host Controller Interface

SCSI
Bus width - 8 bits

Bandwidth - 5 MBps

Max cable length - 6m

Max num device - 8

Fast SCSI

Bus width - 8 bits

Bandwidth - 10 MBps

Max cable length - 3m

Max num device - 8

Fast Wide SCSI

Bus width - 16 bits

Bandwidth - 20 MBps

Max cable length - 6m

Max num device - 15

Ultra SCSI

Bus width - 8 bits

Bandwidth - 20 MBps

Max cable length - 3m

Max num device - 8

Ultra Wide SCSI

Bus width - 16 bits

Bandwidth - 40 MBps

Max cable length - 3m

Max num device - 8

Ultra2/LVD
Bus width - 8 bits

Bandwidth - 40 MBps

Max cable length - 12m

Max num device - 8

Ultra2 Wide
Bus width - 16 bits

Bandwidth - 80 MBps

Max cable length - 12m

Max num device - 16

Ultra3
Bus width - 16 bits

Bandwidth - 160 MBps

Max cable length - 12m

Max num device - 16

Ultra-320
Bus width - 16 bits

Bandwidth - 320 MBps

Max cable length - 12m

Max num device - 16

Ultra-640
Bus width - 16 bits

Bandwidth - 640 MBps

Max cable length - 12m

Max num device - 16

SAS
Serial Attached SCSI

Bus width - 1 bits

Bandwidth - 300 MBps

Max cable length - 8m

Max num device - 16.384

SE SCSI
single end SCSI schema

used for slower and shorter cables

differential SCSI aka HVD
HVD - high voltage differential

the line are paired and the signal on one line is electric opposite of the other

Ultra SCSI2
refines HVD scheme by reducing the voltage form +/- 5v to +/-3.3v

iSCSI
internet SCSI

implements SCSI cmds and protocols across an ethernet network. Provides location independent storage

VL or VLB
Vesa Local Bus

AoE
ATA over Ethernet, a protocol that enables access to SATA devices over an Ethernet physical layer

iSCSI
SCSI over TCP/IP

SAS
Serial attached SCSI, which permits SCSI connectivity over cables up to 8 meter long

HyperSCSI
SCSI over Ethernet

FCP

FCoE

iFCP

SANoIP
Fiber Channel Protocol

a mapping of SCSI over Fiber Channel

FCoE - Fiber Channel over Ethernet

iFCP - Fiber Channel over IP

SANoIP - Fiber Channel over IP

WORM
write once, read many (Good for an offsite backup method that is replicated and needs to guarantee that the
data cannot be changed once it is replicated)

RAID 0
stripping

Data is divided into blocks, and the blocks are distributed across the drives in the array

Improves speed no data redundancy

RAID 1
mirroring/duplexing

Data is duplicated onto a second disk.

Provides data redundancy.

No performance improvement

RAID 1 mirroring

RAID 1 duplexing
mirroring - Single controller

duplexing - Two controllers

RAID 2
An array of disks in which the data is striped at the bit level across all disks in the array. Error correction info is stored on multiple parity disks.

High performance improvement

Recover single bit error

RAID 3
stripping with parity

Data is striped byte by byte onto separate drives.

Parity is stores on an additional, dedicated parity disk.

Provides improvement when large chucks of data are accessed (video)

RAID 4
similar to RAID 3, except that data is striped by the block rather than by the byte.

High read performance when working with small files

RAID 5
striping with distributed parity

Data is divided into an even number of blocks. These blocks along with an additional parity block are stored across an odd number of disk.

Provides performance improvement as data can be written and read at the same time

RAID 6
similar to RAID 5 except that there are two parity bits instead of 1

RAID 0+1
Drive are striped and then mirrored. Min of 4 drives.

You create the striped arrays one of which becomes the mirror of the data

   RAID1

+-----------+

RAID0   RAID0

RAID 1+1
An array in which data is both mirrored and striped simultaneously. RAID 1 mirrored set of drives is then stripped to provide fault tolerance and high performance. Implemented with 4 drives

RAID0

+-------------+

RAID1   RAID1

RAID 50
data is striped at block level across multiple RAID 5 arrays.

Better fault tolerance than either RAID0 or RAID5

RAID0

+-------------+

RAID5   RAID5

hypervisor
virtual managers

the core virtualization software that enables multiple virtual computers to run on a single physical host

bare metal hypervisor
is one you install directly on the server's hardware

host-based hypervisor
one that runs within an operating system - install the OS first and the install the hypervisor

authentication
positive identification of the entity, that wants to access info or service that have been secured

authorization

the sate in which a predetermined level of access is granted to the entity so that it can access the resource

accounting

tracking of user's actions

NOS

NDS

network directory service

network operating system

Wide SCSI

Bus Width (bits) - 16

Bus Frequency (MHz) - 5

Transfer Rate (Mb/s) - 10

Cable type - 68-pin

Signaling type - SE & HVD

Max. devices - 16

Max. cable length - 6m(SE) & 25m(HVD)

Fast SCSI

Bus Width (bits) - 8

Bus Frequency (MHz) - 10

Transfer Rate (Mb/s) - 10

Cable type - 50-pin

Signaling type - SE & HVD

Max. devices - 8

Max. cable length - 3m(SE) & 25m(HVD)

Fast Wide SCSI
Bus Width (bits) - 16

Bus Frequency (MHz) - 10

Transfer Rate (Mb/s) - 20

Cable type - 68-pin

Signaling type - SE & HVD

Max. devices - 16

Max. cable length - 3m(SE) & 25m(HVD)

ULTRA
Bus Width (bits) - 8

Bus Frequency (MHz) - 20

Transfer Rate (Mb/s) - 20

Cable type - 50-pin

Signaling type - SE & HVD

Max. devices - 8(4 if 3m max length)

Max. cable length - 1.5m(SE) & 25m(HVD)

Wide ULTRA

Bus Width (bits) - 16

Bus Frequency (MHz) - 20

Transfer Rate (Mb/s) - 40

Cable type - 68-pin

Signaling type - SE & HVD

Max. devices - 8(4 if 3m max length)

Max. cable length - 1.5m(SE) & 25m(HVD)

Ultra 2

Bus Width (bits) - 8

Bus Frequency (MHz) - 40

Transfer Rate (Mb/s) - 40

Cable type - 50-pin

Signaling type - LVD & HVD

Max. devices - 8(2 if 25m max length LVD)

Max. cable length - 1.5m(SE) & 25m(HVD)

Wide Ultra 2

Bus Width (bits) - 16

Bus Frequency (MHz) - 40

Transfer Rate (Mb/s) - 80

Cable type - 68-pin

Signaling type - LVD & HVD

Max. devices - 16(2 if 25m max length LVD)

Max. cable length - 1.5m(SE) & 25m(HVD)

LPD

CUPS

LPD - Line Printer Deamon

CUPS - Common Unix Printin System

SNMP v3 important feature

Message integrity

Authentication

Encryption

MIB

MIB - management information DB

a hierarchical DB of info managed by an agent

WBEM
web-based enterprise management

standard-based architecture for application and systems management.

WMI
Windows Management Instrumentation

Windows Management Instrumentation (WMI)
is the infrastructure for management data and operations on Windows-based operating systems. You can write WMI scripts or applications to automate administrative tasks on remote computers but WMI also supplies management data to other parts of the operating system and products, for example System Center Operations Manager

QIC
quarter-inch cartridge

belt driven, tape needs to be re tensioned periodically

DAT
digital audio tape

designed for audio recording. Contains two read heads and two write heads

DLT
digital linear tape

Liner serpentine recording with multiple tracks on 12.6mm wide tape

SDLT

Super DLT is a higher-capacity version of DLT. Capacities range from 15 GB to 1200 GB

LTO

linear tape open

2 type

Accelis - 8'' tape and dual-reel cartridge

Ultrium - .5" tape and a single-reel cartridge

AIT

advanced intelligent tape

8mm tape in a 3.5" drive - 20 to 400 GB

SAIT

Super AIT - uses 0.5" single-rail 500 to 1000gb

dib

dual independent bus

process architecture that includes two buses: one to the main system memory and another to the L2 cache

front side bus

the speed at which the processor interacts with the rest of the system

hyperthreading
an Intel technology that enables a single processor to execute two streams of instructions at the same time, as if it were two processors

multimedia extensions (MMX)
an expanded set of instructions supported by a processor that provides multimedia specific functions

pipelining
the overlapping of the steps involved in processing instructions

SMID
single instruction multiple data

technique by which a single instruction can be applied to more than one piece of data

superscalar
a technique that enables a processor to execute more than one instruction in a single clock cycle

nx
no execute

enables the cpu to mark a section of memory as non-executable

NX is XS Execute Disable by Intel

Enhanced Virus Protection by AMDN

buffer overflow attacks

virus writes overfill an area of data storage, eventually placing executable code within your pc memory

stepping

version indicator within a processor line

pdip

pga

pdip - plastic dual inline package

pga - pin grid array

cpga

spga

cpga - ceramic ping grid array

spga - staggered pin grid array

ppga

fc-pga

ppga - plastic pin grid array

fc-pga - flip chip grid array

LMIC

locally managed internet connections

asmp
asymmetrical multiprocessing
specific jobs are assigned to specific processors

bus snooping
permits a processor to monitor the memory addresses placed on the system bus by other devices/ The snooping processor is looking for memory addresses on the system that it has cached. When matched, it writes the values of those memory address from its cache to the system memory

mpp
massively parallel processing

granularity
determines the maximum number of kernel threads that can be run concurrently

Which of the following items is not considered important when matching characteristics for additional Intel microprocessor on SMP-capable server boards?

1)Family

2)Stepping

3)Model

4)Cache
4)Cache

The cache memory is not considered when matching characteristics between processors on SMP server boards

NOS is capable of running multiple CPU after installing a new CPU the system boots without recognizing it?

1)Configure NOS for SMP

2)Replace bad CPU

3)Examine the stepping of new CPU

4)Perform BIOS upgrade
1)Configure NOS for SMP

the most likely cause of the problem is that NOS is not properly configured to provide SMP support

Select most accurate statement:

1)SMP systems are more expensive to implement than ASMP

2)SMP is easier to implement than ASMP

3)SMP is a slower implementation than ASMP

4)In an SMP server system, all CPUs share the same board, but require their own memory, peripherals and NOS
2)SMP is easier to implement than ASMP

SMP is less expensive than ASMP

SMP is faster than a single CPU solution

Raid and SCSI

SCSI bus

SCSI bus refers to the physical path that is used to transfer data. The two types of SCSI busses used are 8-bit and 16-bit. The 8-bit bus, which is also known as the narrow bus, uses a 50-pin connector. The 16-bit bus, which is also known as the wide bus, uses a 68-pin connector.

HBA

The Host Bus Adapter, or HBA, is a SCSI card that acts as an interface between SCSI and the computer.

Daisy chain

A daisy chain is a series of devices connected to a single SCSI bus.

SCSI ID

Each device in a daisy chain is allocated a unique ID, known as SCSI ID, for easy identification.

LUN

In some devices, each independent unit within the device is allocated a unique Logical Unit Number, or LUN, for easy identification.

Terminator

A terminator is a resistors connected to the end of a SCSI bus to neutralize reflected pulses that cause data loss.

Target

A target is a device connected to a SCSI bus.

what does RAID stand for?
Redundant Array of Independent disks (used to be inexpensive disks)

what techniques does a RAID system use to improve data read/write and /or performance?
striping, mirroring, and parity

what is RAID striping?
a technique where RAID splits data into multiple blocks and stores each block on separate hard disks. This improves the speed at which the data is read and written. Unlike a single hard disk where the processor can read or write only one block at a time, multiple hard disks enable the processor to simultaneously read or write multiple blocks of data.

what is RAID mirroring?
a technique where RAID provides redundancy by storing the same data on two different hard disks. The two hard disks that store the data are known as a mirrored pair. Mirroring protects an organization from data loss and downtime - if a hard disk fails, the server can continue to access data from the other hard disk.

what is RAID parity?
Parity, like mirroring, is a redundancy technique that enables you to recover data in the event of a hard disk failure. The difference is that unlike mirroring, which stores a duplicate set of data, parity stores only a mathematical construct of data. This mathematical construct, which needs less disk space than regular data, can be used to reconstruct data when a disk fails.

What are the features of RAID?
It provides redundant copies of data
It splits data across multiple hard disks

RAID controller
whether independent, integrated, or external - has built-in software called firmware on it. Firmware helps the controller to manage the hard disk array and enable striping, mirroring, and parity.

what ways can you implement Hardware RAID?
PCI RAID controller card

The most widely used hardware device for enabling RAID is the PCI RAID controller card. You connect this card to the PCI slot on the server's motherboard.

a motherboard with an integrated RAID controller, or

You can also enable RAID by using a motherboard with an integrated RAID controller, which usually provides the same features as an independent controller. Using an integrated controller is cheaper than using a PCI controller, but it doesn't provide the option of changing or upgrading the card.

external RAID storage

Another way of enabling RAID is by using external RAID storage, which uses a separate enclosure to store hard disks and has its own RAID controllers. It's connected to the server through a SCSI interface and is the most expensive method of implementing RAID.

write-caching
To accelerate the speed at which data is written to and retrieved from a RAID array, you can enable a method known as write-caching With write-caching, new data is written not only to the hard disks but also to the cache of the RAID controller. Using the cache helps decrease the time it takes to write and retrieve data. This is because data can be written to or read from the cache 1,000 times faster than from a disk.

what methods can you use to implement write-caching?
write-back caching or

When you use write-back caching, the server is notified that the write transaction is complete as soon as data is written to the cache. This allows the server to immediately proceed to its next task. After some time, the data is transferred permanently to the disks.

This is a quick caching method because it saves time by enabling the server to immediately move on to its next task without waiting for data to be written to the disks. However, this method is also risky because it increases the chances of losing data in the event of a power failure. If you lose power before the data is transferred from the cache to the disk, you permanently lose that data. The application that created the data cannot recover it because the controller would have notified the server that the data was written to the disks.

write-through caching

When you use write-through caching, new data is stored both to the cache and the disk before the server is notified that the write transaction is complete.

This caching method is slower than write-back caching because the server has to wait for data to be written to both the cache and disks before it can move on to its next task. However, this method is also safer than write-back caching. If you lose power before the data is written to the hard disks, the application that created the data can help in recovering it. This is because the controller wouldn't have notified the server that the data was written to the disks.

what are the disadvantages to software RAID?
slows server performance

Unlike Hardware RAID, where a controller enables RAID, Software RAID consumes large amounts of memory and processing power to enable RAID, slowing the performance of the server.

Additionally, because the operating system has to be booted to enable Software RAID, you cannot boot the operating system from the RAID array. You need to create a separate partition for the operating system. This consumes disk space on the array, increases boot time, and further slows the overall performance.

supports limited RAID implementations

Unlike Hardware RAID that supports all RAID implementations, Software RAID supports only a limited amount of RAID implementations.

increases security issues, and

An operating system is more vulnerable to bugs and attacks than the firmware of a controller, so using Software RAID exposes the disk array to security issues.

doesn't support multiple operating systems

Software RAID doesn't support a multiple operating system environment. This is because only the operating system that enables Software RAID can access the disk array; other operating systems cannot access it.

To avoid downtime when replacing failed disks, organizations use
hot plug disks

A hot plug disk is a special hard disk that can be installed and uninstalled without shutting down a server.

hot swaps

A hot swap enables a RAID system to recognize when a hot plug disk has been installed or uninstalled from a server. When a hot plug disk is installed, a hot swap automatically downloads the data normally stored on a failed disk onto the new disk.

For example, when a hot plug disk is installed on a RAID 0 system, hot swap automatically downloads data from the failed disk's mirror onto it. Similarly, in a RAID 5 system, hot swap automatically reconstructs the data from the failed disk and restores it on the newly installed hot plug disk.

hot spares, and

A hot spare is a spare hard disk that is used as a replacement for a failed disk. It enables the RAID system to function normally in case of a disk failure. You can replace a failed disk with a hot spare manually, or configure the system to automatically use a hot spare when a disk fails. After a failed disk is replaced with a hot spare, you can buy a new disk, copy data from the hot spare onto it, and make the hot spare available for future use. Alternatively, you may keep the hot spare as the replacement disk and configure a new hard disk to be used as a hot spare in the future.

fail over

Fail over is used in RAID implementations that use mirroring. When a disk fails, this technique enables a RAID system to automatically use its mirror disk until it is replaced.

RAID 0

requires two or more hard disks, uses striping to improve system performance. It doesn't use either mirroring or parity to provide data redundancy. (By not providing data redundancy, RAID 0 uses all system resources for reading and writing striped data. This makes it the fastest performing RAID implementation. It's also the most inexpensive implementation because it doesn't need storage space to store redundant data The disadvantage of RAID 0 is that the failure of even a single hard disk results in the permanent loss of all data. This is because each hard disk in a RAID 0 array stores only partial striped data. When one hard disk fails, the partial data in the other hard disks becomes unusable

RAID 1

Requires at least two hard disks, uses mirroring to save the same data across several hard disks. An advantage of using RAID 1 is that there is no downtime in the event of a disk failure. When a disk fails, users can continue to access lost data from its mirror disk. Another advantage of RAID 1 is that it enables the server to read data from multiple hard disks, thus improving the overall performance. By using mirroring instead of parity, it also writes redundant data faster because it doesn't need to calculate parity information

RAID 1 disadvantages

A limitation of RAID 1 is that it is expensive to implement. It requires you to have twice the storage capacity you need - half for storing data and half for duplicating it. Another disadvantage is that it's performance is slower than RAID 0 because it doesn't't use striping.

RAID 3

a RAID implementation that provides both data redundancy and high performance by using parity and striping. A RAID 3 implementation uses three or more disks, where one hard disk is used to store parity information.

RAID 3 advantages

An advantage of RAID 3 is that it's cheaper to implement than RAID 1 because parity requires less disk space to store redundant data. Another advantage of RAID 3 is that it always reads and writes complete instead of partial data stripes, which makes it useful for transferring large amounts of data.

RAID 3 Disadvantages

A drawback of RAID 3 is that the dedicated parity disk offsets some performance advantages of striping. When data is written to multiple disks, the dedicated parity disk cannot simultaneously calculate parity information for each disk. This creates a bottleneck in the parity disk that slows down the server. Another disadvantage is that when a disk fails, its data cannot be accessed immediately. It can only be accessed after the data is reconstructed using information from the parity disk.

RAID 5

provides both high performance and redundancy using striping and parity. To implement RAID 5, you need a minimum of three disks. RAID 5 addresses the performance issues of RAID 3 while retaining its advantages such as low redundancy cost. Unlike RAID 3, RAID 5 stores parity information across all disks instead of on a dedicated disk. This enables it to simultaneously write parity information on multiple disks without slowing down the server. RAID 5 also stores striped data differently than RAID 3. RAID 3 stores striped data across a single strip. That is, it stores striped data in the same spot on every disk in the array. RAID 5, however, stores striped data in logical blocks. This accelerates read operations because an application doesn't have to access multiple disks to read data.

RAID 5 disadvantages

RAID 5, like RAID 3, is that the data of a failed disk cannot be accessed immediately. It can only be accessed after it has been reconstructed and stored on a new hard disk.

RAID 6

an advanced RAID implementation that functions like RAID 5. The only difference is that it provides additional fault tolerance by storing two copies of parity information across all disks. The redundant parity information is useful in cases when two hard disks fail at the same time. However, to store the redundant copy of parity information, RAID 6 requires a minimum of four disks.

Hybrid RAID levels

A hybrid RAID level is a combination of two RAID levels. Some commonly used hybrid RAID levels are as follows:

RAID 0+1

RAID 1+0, and

RAID 50

RAID 0+1, a hybrid of RAID 0 and RAID 1, uses striping and mirroring to provide both high performance and redundancy. It requires at least two sets of hard disks, with each set containing at least two hard disks. To store data, RAID 0+1 stripes it into blocks and stores the blocks across each disk in the first set. It then uses mirroring to copy the striped data from the first set onto the other sets.

A market research company wants to protect archived research reports stored on its server against disk failure. These reports are not accessed frequently. Also, the company has a limited budget and doesn't want to use too much storage space to store redundant data. Which RAID level should it use?

Options:

RAID 0

RAID 1

RAID 5

RAID 0+1

uses parity to provide data redundancy. Parity requires less space to enable data redundancy because it uses a mathematical construct to restore lost data.

A multimedia company uses a server to store files for an animation project. To meet deadlines, it wants its animators to be able to quickly access and edit these files from the server. Because it has a small IT budget, the company doesn't want data redundancy. Instead, it will make frequent backups on optical disks. Which RAID level should it use?

Options:

RAID 0

RAID 1

RAID 3

RAID 5
RAID 0

is inexpensive and uses striping to enable quick read/write performance. It's also the fastest RAID implementation because it doesn't use server resources for mirroring and parity.

A customer support department needs to quickly access large volumes of customer data stored on its servers. As a 24-hour

service, it also needs data to be constantly available. Additionally, it wants to store two copies of all data to protect it against disk failure. Which RAID level should this department use?

Options:

RAID 0

RAID 5

RAID 0+1

RAID 3
RAID 0+1

uses RAID 0 to provide fast access to data and RAID 1 to enable redundancy and provide continuous access to data.

A public company stores monthly performance reports on some of its servers. Although these reports are not accessed frequently, they're critical files. The company wants them to be protected even when two disks fail at the same time. Which RAID level should it use?
RAID 6 stores two sets of parity information. This enables it to protect data when two disks fail at the same time.

RAID 0
(Striping) Offers low cost and maximum performance, but offers no fault tolerance; a single disk failure results in TOTAL data loss. Businesses use RAID 0 mainly for tasks requiring fast access to a large capacity of temporary disk storage (such as video/audio post-production, multimedia imaging, CAD, data logging, etc.) where in case of a disk failure, the data can be easily reloaded without impacting the business. There are also no cost disadvantages as all storage is usable. RAID 0 usable capacity is 100% as all available drives are used

RAID 1

(Mirroring) Provides cost-effective, high fault tolerance for configurations with two disk drives. RAID 1 refers to maintaining duplicate sets of all data on separate disk drives. It also provides the highest data availability since two complete copies of all information are maintained. There must be two disks in the configuration and there is a cost disadvantage as the usable capacity is half the number of available disks. RAID 1 offers data protection insurance for any environments where absolute data redundancy, availability and performance are key, and cost per usable gigabyte of capacity is a secondary consideration.

RAID 1 usable capacity is 50% of the available drives in the RAID set.

RAID 1E

(Striped Mirroring) Combines data striping from RAID 0 with data mirroring from RAID 1. Data written in a stripe on one disk is mirrored to a stripe on the next drive in the array. The main advantage over RAID 1 is that RAID 1E arrays can be implemented using an odd number of disks.

RAID 1E usable capacity is 50% of the total available capacity of all disk drives in the RAID set.

RAID 5

(Striping with Parity) Uses data striping in a technique designed to provide fault-tolerant data storage, but doesn't require duplication of data like RAID 1 and RAID 1E. Data is striped across all of the drives in the array, but for each stripe through the array (one stripe unit from each disk) one stripe unit is reserved to hold parity data calculated from the other stripe units in the same stripe. Read performance is therefore very good, but there is a penalty for writes, since the parity data has to be recalculated and written along with the new data. To avoid a bottleneck, the parity data for consecutive stripes is interleaved with the data across all disks in the array.

RAID 5 has been the standard in server environments requiring fault tolerance. The RAID parity requires one disk drive per RAID set, so usable capacity will always be one disk drive les than the number of available disks in the configuration of available capacity - still better than RAID 1 which as only a 50% usable capacity.

RAID 5 requires a minimum of three disks and a maximum of 16 disks to be implemented. RAID 5 usable capacity is between 67% - 94%, depending on the number of data drives in the RAID set.

RAID 5EE

Provides the protection of RAID 5 with higher I/Os per second by utilizing one more drive, with data efficiently distributed across the spare drive for improved I/O access.

RAID 5EE distributes the hot-spare drive space over the N+1 drives comprising the RAID-5 array plus standard hot-spare drive. This means that in normal operating mode the hot spare is an active participant in the array rather than spinning unused. In a normal RAID 5 array adding a hot-spare drive to RAID 5 array protects data by reducing the time spent in the critical rebuild state. This technique does not make maximum use of the hot-spare drive because it sits idle until a failure occurs. Often many years can elapse before the hot-spare drive is ever used. For small RAID 5 arrays in particular, having an extra disk to read from (four disks instead of three, as an example) can provide significantly better read performance.

RAID 6

(Striping with dual parity) Data is striped across several physical drives and dual parity is used to store and recover data. It tolerates the failure of two drives in an array, providing better fault tolerance than RAID 5. It also enables the use of more cost-effective ATA and SATA disks to storage business critical data.

This RAID level is similar to RAID 5, but includes a second parity scheme that is distributed across different drives and therefore offers extremely high fault tolerance and drive failure tolerance. RAID 6 can withstand a double disk failure.

RAID 6 requires a minimum of four disks and a maximum of 16 disks to be implemented. Usable capacity is always 2 less than the number of available disk drives in the RAID set.

RAID 10

is a stripe of mirrors. Required 4 drives, also known as RAID 1+0.
 Definition: Raid 0 array of mirrors(2 or 3 way mirrors).   Combines RAID 0

striping and RAID 1 mirroring. This level provides the improved performance of striping while still providing the redundancy of mirroring.

RAID 10 is the result of forming a RAID 0 array from two or more RAID 1 arrays. This RAID level provides fault tolerance - up to one disk of each sub-array may fail without causing loss of data.

Usable capacity of RAID 10 is 50% of available disk drives.

RAID 50

A RAID 50 combines the straight block-level striping of RAID 0 with the distributed parity of RAID 5. This is a RAID 0 array striped across RAID 5 elements. It requires at least 6 drives. Combines multiple RAID 5 sets with RAID 0 (striping). Striping helps to increase capacity and performance without adding disks to each RAID 5 array (which will decrease data availability and could impact performance when running in a degraded mode).

RAID 50 comprises RAID 0 striping across lower-level RAID 5 arrays. The benefits of RAID 5 are gained while the spanned RAID 0 allows the incorporation of many more disks into a single logical drive. Up to one drive in each sub-array may fail without loss of data. Also, rebuild times are substantially less then a single large RAID 5 array.

Usable capacity of RAID 50 is between 67% - 94%, depending on the number of data drives in the RAID set.

Motherboards

Motherboard
allows all the parts of your computer to receive power and communicate with one another

Form Factor
The shape and layout of a motherboard. Affects where individual components go and the shape of the computer's case

Socket for the Microprocessor

Determines what kind of Central Processing Unit (CPU) the motherboard uses.

Chipset
Part of the motherboard's logic system and is usually made of two parts -- the northbridge and the southbridge. These two "bridges" connect the CPU to other parts of the computer.

Basic Input/Output System (BIOS) Chip
Controls the most basic functions of the computer and performs a self-test every time you turn it on.

Real Time Clock Chip
A battery-operated chip that maintains basic settings and the system time.

Peripheral Component Interconnect (PCI)
Connections for video, sound and video capture cards, as well as network cards

Accelerated Graphics Port (AGP)
Dedicated port for video cards.

Integrated Drive Electronics (IDE)
Interfaces for the hard drives

Universal Serial Bus or FireWire
External peripherals

Redundant Array of Independent Discs (RAID) Controllers

Allow the computer to recognize multiple drives as one drive.

PCI Express
A newer protocol that acts more like a network than a bus. It can eliminate the need for other ports, including the AGP port.

On-board Sound, Networking, Video or Other Peripheral Support
Rather than relying on plug-in cards

Pin Grid Array (PGA)
In the early days of PC computers, all processors had the same set of pins that would connect the CPU to the motherboard

Socket 7
Pins would fit into a socket layout

Socket 478
For older Pentium and Celeron processors

Socket 754
For AMD Sempron and some AMD Athlon processors

Socket 939
For newer and faster AMD Athlon processors

Socket AM2
For the newest AMD Athlon processors

Socket A
For older AMD Athlon processors

Land Grid Array (LGD) or Socket T
Different from a PGA in that the pins are actually part of the socket, not the CPU

Northbridge
Connects directly to the processor via the front side bus (FSB). A memory controller is located on the northbridge, which gives the CPU fast access to the memory. Also connects to the AGP or PCI Express bus and to the memory itself.

Southbridge
Slower than the northbridge, and information from the CPU has to go through the northbridge before reaching the southbridge.

Bus
A circuit that connects one part of the motherboard to another. The more data a bus can handle at one time, the faster it allows information to travel.

Speed of the Bus
Measured in megahertz (MHz), refers to how much data can move across the bus simultaneously.

Front Side Bus (FSB)
Connects the CPU to the northbridge. FSB speeds can range from 66 MHz to over 800 MHz.

Back Side Bus

Connects the CPU with the level 2 (L2) cache, also known as secondary or external cache. The processor determines the speed of the back side bus.

Memory Bus

Connects the northbridge to the memory.

IDE or ATA Bus

Connects the southbridge to the disk drives.

AGP Bus

Connects the video card to the memory and the CPU. The speed of the AGP bus is usually 66 MHz.

PCI Bus

Connects PCI slots to the southbridge. On most systems, the speed of the PCI bus is 33 MHz.

PCI Express

Is much faster than PCI but is still compatible with current software and operating systems. PCI Express is likely to replace both PCI and AGP busses.

TCP/IP

DoD Model
Process/Application layer, Host-to-Host layer, Internet layer, Network Access layer

Process/Application layer
Application, Presentation, and Session layers

Host-to-Host layer
Transport layer

Internet layer
Network layer

Network Access layer
Data Link and Physical layers

Process/Application Layer Protocols
Telnet, FTP, TFTP, NFS, SMTP, LDP, X Window, SNMP, DNS, DHCP/BootP

Telnet
terminal emulation - allows a user on a remote client machine, called the Telnet client, to access the resources of another machine, the Telnet server

File Transfer Protocol (FTP)
file transfer between 2 machines, a protocol and a program, accesses directories and files, uses Telnet for login, cannot execute remote programs

Trivial File Transfer Protocol (TFTP)

stripped-down version of FTP, no directory-browsing abilities, uses smaller blocks of data, no authentication

Network File System (NFS)

allows two different types of file systems to interoperate

Simple Mail Transfer Protocol (SMTP)

uses a spooled, or queued, method of mail delivery, used to send mail (POP3 is used to receive mail)

Line Printer Daemon (LPD)

designed for printer sharing, along with the Line Printer (LPR) program, allows print jobs to be spooled and sent to the network's printers using TCP/IP

X Window

to allow a program, called a client, to run on one computer and have it display things through a window server on another computer

Simple Network Management Protocol (SNMP)

collects and manipulates network information,

Baseline

a report delimiting the operational traits of a healthy network

Trap

Alerts sent by SNMP agents

Domain Name Service (DNS)

resolves hostnames/fully qualified domain name (FQDN)

Dynamic Host Configuration Protocol (DHCP)
provides an IP Address, Subnet Mask, Domain Name, Default Gateway, DNS, WINS

Bootstrap Protocol (BootP)
gives an IP address to a host but the host's hardware address must be entered manually in a BootP table; used to send 'diskless workstations' their boot image

DHCP
connectionless, uses User Datagram Protocol (UDP)

Host-to-Host Layer Protocols
Transmission Control Protocol (TCP) & User Datagram Protocol (UDP)

TCP
segments and sequences information, waits for acknowledgments over the virtual circuit

TCP
full-duplex, connection-oriented, reliable, and accurate

TCP
lots of overhead

TCP Header

Source Port, Destination Port, Sequence Number, Acknowledgment Number, Header Number, Reserved, Code Bits, Window, Checksum, Urgent, Options, Data

Source port
The port number of the application on the host sending the data

Destination port
The port number of the application requested on the destination host

Sequence number
Puts the data back in the correct order or retransmits missing or damaged data, a process called sequencing

Acknowledgment number
Defines which TCP octet is expected next

Header length
The number of 32-bit words in the TCP header. This indicates where the data begins.

Reserved
Always set to zero

Code bits
Control functions used to set up and terminate a session

Window
The window size the sender is willing to accept, in octets

Checksum
cyclic redundancy check (CRC) checks the header and data fields

Urgent
The urgent pointer points to the sequence number of the octet following the urgent data

Options
May be 0 or a multiple of 32 bits

Data
Handed down to the TCP protocol at the Transport layer

UDP
fast, connectionless, unreliable

UDP Segment
Source Port, Destination Port, Length, Checksum, Data

Port Numbers below 1024
considered well-known port numbers dynamically assigned by the source host

Port Numbers 1024 and above
used by the upper layers to set up sessions with other hosts, used by TCP to use as source and destination addresses

Port 23
Telnet, TCP

Port 25
SMTP, TCP

Port 80
HTTP, TCP

Port 21
FTP, TCP

Port 53
DNS, TCP & UDP

Port 443
HTTPS, TCP

Port 161
SNMP, UDP

Port 69
TFTP, UDP

Port 110
POP3, UDP

Port 119

News, UDP

Internet Layer Protocols
Internet Protocol (IP), Internet Control Message Protocol (ICMP), Address Resolution Protocol (ARP), Reverse Address Resolution Protocol (RARP), Proxy ARP

Internet Protocol (IP)
decides where a packet is to be sent next, choosing the best path using a routing table

IP Header
Version, Header Length, Priority & Type, Total Length, Identification, Flags, Fragment Offset, Time to Live, Protocol, Header Checksum, Source IP, Destination IP, Options, Data

Version
IP Version number

Header Length
HLEN in 32-bit words

Priority & Type
how the datagram should be handled

Total Length
Length of of the packet

Identification

Unique IP-packet value

Flags
Specifies whether fragmentation should occur

Fragment offset
Provides fragmentation and reassembly if the packet is too large to put in a frame

Time to Live
Kills packets when time expires

Protocol
Port of upper-layer protocol (TCP is port 6 or UDP is port 17 [hex])

Header checksum
Cyclic redundancy check (CRC) on header only

Source IP
IP address of sending station

Destination IP
32-bit IP address of the station this packet is destined for

Options
Used for network testing, debugging, security, and more

Data

Upper-layer data

Internet Protocol (IP)
the Internet layer; the other protocols found here merely exist to support it

Port 6 (hex)
TCP

Port 17 (hex)
UDP

Internet Control Message Protocol (ICMP)
management protocol and messaging service provider for IP

Internet Control Message Protocol (ICMP)
They can provide hosts with information about network problems

Internet Control Message Protocol (ICMP)
They are encapsulated within IP datagrams

ICMP events and messages
Destination Unreachable, Buffer Full, Hops, Ping, Traceroute,

Destination Unreachable
When a router can't send an IP datagram any further

Buffer Full
When a router's memory buffer for receiving incoming datagrams is full

Hops

Each IP datagram is allotted a certain number of routers, called hops, to pass through. If it reaches its limit of hops before arriving at its destination, the last router to receive that datagram deletes it. The executioner router then uses ICMP to send an obituary message, informing the sending machine of the demise of its datagram

Ping (Packet Internet Groper)

Used to check the physical and logical connectivity of machines on an internetwork

Traceroute

Used to discover the path a packet takes as it traverses an internetwork

Reverse Address Resolution Protocol (RARP)

discovers the identity of the IP address for diskless machines by sending out a packet that includes its MAC address

Address Resolution Protocol (ARP)

Used to find the hardware address from a known IP address

Proxy Address Resolution Protocol (Proxy ARP)

The technique in which one host, usually a router, answers ARP requests intended for another machine. By "faking" its identity, the router accepts responsibility for routing packets to the "real" destination. Proxy ARP can help machines on a subnet reach remote subnets without the need to configure routing or a default gateway.

IP Address

32-bit logical numeric identifier assigned to each machine on an IP network

Bit
one digit, 1 or 0

Byte
8 bits (with parity)

Octet
8 bits

Network Address/Number
numerical identifier for a remote network; uniquely identifies each network

Broadcast Address
address used by applications and hosts to send information to all nodes on a network

IP Address
may be depicted in dotted-decimal, hex, or binary

Node Address
uniquely identifies each machine on a network

What is the Class C address range in decimal and in binary?
192-223, 110xxxxx

What layer of the DoD model is equivalent to the Transport layer of the OSI model?

Host-to-Host

What is the valid range of a Class A network address?
1-126

What is the 127.0.0.1 address used for?
Loopback or diagnostics

How do you find the network address from a listed IP address?
Turn all host bits off

How do you find the broadcast address from a listed IP address?
Turn all host bits on

What is the Class A private IP address space?
10.0.0.0 through 10.255.255.255

What is the Class B private IP address space?
172.16.0.0 through 172.31.255.255

What is the Class C private IP address space?
192.168.0.0 through 192.168.255.255

What are all the available characters that you can use in hexadecimal addressing?
0-9 and A, B, C, D, E, and F

What is the decimal and hexadecimal equivalent of the binary number 10011101?
157 & 0x9D

Which of the following allows a router to respond to an ARP request that is intended for a remote host?
Proxy ARP

You want to implement a mechanism that automates the IP configuration, including IP address, subnet mask, default gateway, and DNS information. Which protocol will you use to accomplish this?
DHCP

What protocol is used to find the hardware address of a local device?
ARP

Which of the following are layers in the TCP/IP model?
Application, Transport, Internet

Which class of IP address provides a maximum of only 254 host addresses per network ID?
Class C

Which of the following describe the DHCP Discover message?
It uses FF:FF:FF:FF:FF:FF as a layer 2 broadcast; It uses UDP as the Transport layer protocol

Which layer 4 protocol is used for a Telnet connection?
TCP

Which statements are true regarding ICMP packets?
They can provide hosts with information about network problems; They are encapsulated within IP datagrams

Which of the following services use TCP?
SMTP, FTP, HTTP

Which of the following services use UDP?
DHCP, SNMP, TFTP

Which of the following are TCP/IP protocols used at the Application layer of the OSI model?
Telnet, FTP, TFTP

If you use either Telnet or FTP, which is the highest layer you are using to transmit data?
Application

The DoD model (also called the TCP/IP stack) has four layers. Which layer of the DoD model is equivalent to the Network layer of the OSI model?
Internet

Which of the following is a private IP address?
172.20.14.36

What layer in the TCP/IP stack is equivalent to the Transport layer of the OSI model?
Host-to-Host

Which statements are not true regarding ICMP packets?
UDP will send an ICMP Information request message to the source host; ICMP guarantees datagram delivery; ICMP is encapsulated within UDP datagrams

What is the address range of a Class B network address in binary?
10xxxxxx

Which of the following protocols use both TCP and UDP?
DNS

BIOS/CMOS

chipset
extends the data bus to every device on the PC

BIOS
basic input/output services

system BIOS function
supportive services that enable the CPU to communicate with devices

ROM

read-only memory

flash ROM
contents can be updated or changed

system ROM
where the BIOS is stored

firmware
programs stored on ROM chips

software
programs stored on erasable media

system ROM storage capacity
2MB

CMOS
complementary metal-oxide semiconductor

CMOS function
stores information about specific device parameters

location of CMOS on modern systems
Southbridge

CMOS storage capacity
64KB

CMOS setup utility
enables you to access and update CMOS data

location of CMOS setup program
system ROM

two primary BIOS manufacturers
AMI and Phoenix

access CMOS setup
at boot

chassis intrusion detection
trips switch when someone opens the case

TPM
Trusted Platform Module

TPM function
acts as a secure crypto-processor

option ROM
BIOS stored directly on a device (e.g., video card)

legacy terms for the chipset
Northbridge and Southbridge

device driver
file containing the commands to talk to a specific device

Device Manager
utility that allows you to change or remove drivers

POST
power-on self test

POST function
checks system devices at boot

beep codes
indicate POST errors before and during video test

text errors
indicate POST errors after video test

POST card
device used to monitor POST and identify problems

bootstrap loader
locates boot sector and passes control to OS

CMOS battery
allows CMOS to retain its data when PC is turned off

CMOS time/date not set
CMOS battery may need to be replaced

clear CMOS jumper
resets all CMOS settings

flashing the BIOS
updating the system BIOS

EFI
Extensible Firmware Interface

EFI function
a BIOS replacement

UEFI
Unified Extensible Firmware Interface

UEFI function
supersedes original EFI specification

CSM
Compatibility Support Mode

CSM function
supports legacy OS that require traditional BIOS to boot

IRQ, DMA, IOAddr

What are the non changeable IRQ channel?

Channels:

0: System Clock

1: Keyboard

8: Real time clock

IRQ channel 2:

Gateway (Cascade) to IRQ 8-15

IRQ channel 3:
COM 2 and COM 4

IRQ channel 4:
COM 1 and COM 3

IRQ channel 5:
LPT 2 (Often Available and used for sound cards)

IRQ channel 6:
Floppy Drive

IRQ channel 7:
LPT 1

IRQ channel 9:
Redirected as IRQ 2. Also used by USB

IRQ channel 12:
Mouse

IRQ channel 13:
Math Co Processor

IRQ channel 14:
Primary IDE interface

IRQ channel 15:

Secondary IDE interface

What are usual available IRQ channel?
10 and 11(Often used for network cards)

What devices usually use DMA?
Hard drives, CD-ROM drives, Tape drives and Sound cards

Fact: DMA channels
can not be the same for devices

DMA Channel 1:
Sound cards

DMA Channel 2:
Floppy drive

DMA Channel 4:
Secondary DMA Controller

What are the available DMA Channel?
0,3,5,6,7

Fact: Each device in a computer
must have its own I/O address.

COM 1 I/O address range:
3F8 - 3FF

COM 2 I/O address range:
2F8 - 2FF

COM 3 I/O address range:
3E8 - 3EF

COM 4 I/O address range:
2E8 - 2EF

LPT 1 I/O address range:
378 - 37F

LPT 2 I/O address range:
278 - 27F

Floppy Drive I/O address range:
3F0 - 3F7

Sound Card I/O address range:
Often set to base I/O 220

Musical Instrument Digital Interface (MIDI) Port
Often set to base I/O 330

Network Interface Card
Often set to base I/O 300

CPU and Memory

CPU

Abbreviation of central processing unit. The CPU is the brains of the computer. Sometimes referred to simply as the processor or central processor, the CPU is where most calculations take place.

Transistor

An electronic device that can regulate electricity and act as a logical gate or switch for an electrical signal.

Integrated Circuit

Also called chips; multiple transistors integrated into a single module used to store and process bits and bytes in today's computers

Microprocessor

The central processing unit that is generally made from a single integrated circuit.

Registers

Method of temporarily storing or manipulating the data

Clock

- Used to set the pace for all activities inside the computer

-All activities in the computer occur at the same pace as clock pulses

-Motherboard generally has 2 clocks

1. control CPU speed

2. control external data speed

Instruction Sets
- Tell CPU where to find data, when to read data, and what to do with data

- SSE (Streaming SIMD[Single Instruction Multiple Data] Extensions) = 1st enhancement to original

Intel Processors
Main processor company

4 basic elements of processor performance
1. Speed - max number of clock cycles / MHz

2. External Data Bus - data bus size ^ so does the complexity of code that can be transferred between all devices in computer

3. Address Bus - determines max amount of memory addressable by CPU

4. Internal Cache - High speed memory built into processor. A place to store frequently used data

Intel 8088/8086
-1978 1st 16-bit microprocessor

- 1 MB memory

- 8086 too advanced, regressed to 8088

- 8-bit external bus

Numbered Processors

Next three Intel processors after 8088/8086

80286

-1981

- Normal called 286

- Run same apps as 8086 but much faster

-16 MB

- 12 MHz

80386

1. 386DX

 - 32-bit

 - 4 GB

2. 286SX

 - 16-bit configuration

 - easier intro to next gen of computers than DX

80486

- First truly integrated chip

- internal 8k cache

Pentium

- True tech advancement

- 32-bit address & 64-bit data bus

- addition of on board cache

- 2 8KB caches

Pentium Pro

designed for use in servers and workstations

Pentium II

- Housed in new single edge contact (SEC) cartridge

Celeron

-Low cost

-Less powerful

- no cache memory

Pentium III

- Improved clock speeds

Pentium 4

- up to 4GHz

- Slew of new instructions designed to make games, graphics, and calculations faster

Pentium M
Mobile

- Uses core processor of Pentium III

Pentium D
- Represents the end of gigahertz race

- first Dual Core (2 CPUs in same package)

Intel Core
-Allows Symmetric Multiprocessing (SMP) - allows two programs to run at same time

- Hyperthreading - run multiple parts of a program at the same time

Core Duo
- 1st Intel used in Mac

Core 2 Duo
- better efficiency between two cores

Core 2 Quad
- 4 processors in the same package

AMD
Advanced Micro Devices - produce work-alike versions of the Intel processors that became known as clone processors.

Multitasking

- Apparent simultaneous execution of two or more programs by a single processor

- Processor works on one program for an instant, then the next

Cooperative Multitasking
Operating System (OS) transfers control to the programs and programs determine when switching occurs

Preemptive Multitasking
OS controls the switching. OS executes each program for specified time period

Multithreading
Functions of the Operating System: A form of multitasking that runs multiple tasks within a single application simultaneously

 - video and audio at same time

Multiprocessing
The capability of an operating system to use multiple processors in a single computer, usually to process multiple jobs at one time faster than could be performed with a single processor.

Symmetrical multiprocessing
each CPU has equal access to resources, each CPU determines what to run using a standard algorithm

Asymmetrical multiprocessing
the program designer chooses the processor at the time the program is written. This is seldom used in a PC other than in the program code to control some video processors.

Multicore
a CPU that includes more than two microprocessors on a single integrated circuit, sharing a common cache

System Cooling
-Heat is the enemy

-Electronics consume power; power consumption generates heat

Main heat generators
1. CPU

2. Memory

3. Video processor

4. Motherboard chipset

5. Hard Drive

Heatsink
- Draws heat from heat source through conduction

- Special compound is normally used to maximize the thermal transfer from CPU to heatsink

- Usually made of aluminum or copper. Copper works better / Aluminum is cheaper

Passive Heatsink
relies on its mass and natural air movement to cool the fins

Active Heatsink
heatsink that contains a fan

ROM - Read Only Memory
a data storage system in which information can be read, but not changed. This usually includes permanent programs

PROM - Programmable ROM
A ROM which can be programmed by user once, instead of having to be purchased already programmed. Programmed much like a PLA.

EPROM
(computer science) a read-only memory chip that can be erased by ultraviolet light and programmed again with new data

EEPROM
erased by applying a slightly higher than normal voltage to the chip. Unlike the other types, EEPROM can be erased a byte at a time rather than all at once, and then written to. This type of ROM is found in devices like printers. (source:http://www.ecscolorado.com/faqs/rom.htm)

RAM
Random Access Memory; temporary memory. RAM is expandable, and resides on the motherboard.

SRAM
Static Random Access Memory; the type of memory that does not need to be refreshed and that cache memory is made out of.

DRAM

Dynamic Random Access Memory. Slower, volatile store that needs to have a continuous signal to refresh the contents of the chip

SDRAM

A form of DRAM that utilizes a synchronous interface. It can accept one command and transfer one word of data per clock cycle with typical internal clock frequencies being 100 to 133 MHz.

SIMM

(Single Inline Memory Module)

type of memory module form factor used in the early 1980s to the late 1990s. It was available in 30 pin - (8 bit data rate) and 72 pin - (32 bit data rate) varieties.

DIMM

[Dual In-line Memory Module] These modules have separate electrical contacts on each side of the module enabling a higher density of components.

RIMM

Rambus Inline Memory Module, Industry Standard for RDRAM, 32-bit bus length. Must be installed in pairs/into all available memory slots.

DDR SDRAM

A form of SDRAM that has a double data rate. Its prefix refers to the ability of the memory to achieve a higher bandwidth by transferring data on the rising and falling edges of clock signal. It can be found with the designator of 2, 3, or 4 depending on the clock rate and voltage requirements.

DDR2

it is designed to transfer data at half the clock rate of DDR memory. what this means is for the same number of memory chock cycles it is now possible to move twice as much data as before.

DDR3
moves data at 8x the rate of SDRAM; while reducing the power requirement by 30% as compared to DDR2

internal cache
-L1, integrated into processor chip

-fastest memory in computer

external cache
-L2, external to processor

-2nd fastest memory

Physical Security

Mantrap
A preventive physical control with two doors. Each door requires a separate form of authentication to open

Bollard
A post designed to stop a car, typically deployed in front of building entrances

Smart card
A physical access control device containing an integrated circuit

Tailgating
Following an authorized person into a building without providing

credentials

PERIMETER DEFENSES
Perimeter defenses help prevent, detect, and correct unauthorized physical access.

Fences
Fences may range from simple deterrents such as 3-foot/1 meter-tall fencing to preventive devices, such as an 8-foot 2.4 meter tall fence with barbed wire on top.

Gates
Gates should be placed at controlled points at the perimeter. Secure sites use fences and topography to steer traffic to these points.

Gates
Class I gates deter access. Class IV prevent cars from crashing through.

Bollards
A traffic bollard is a strong post designed to stop a car.

Types of Vehicle Gates
Class I Residential (home use)

Class II Commercial/General Access (parking garage)

Class III Industrial/Limited Access (loading dock for 18-wheeler trucks)

Class IV Restricted Access (airport or prison)

Lights
Lights can act as both a detective and deterrent control. A light which allows a guard to see an intruder is acting as a detective control.

Closed Circuit Television CCTV
is a detective device used to aid guards in

detecting the presence of intruders in restricted areas.

Locks
Locks are a preventive physical security control, used on doors and windows to prevent unauthorized physical access.

Locks
Locks may be mechanical, such as key locks or combination locks, or electronic, which are often used with smart cards or magnetic stripe cards.

Key locks
Key locks require a physical key to unlock. Keys may be shared or sometimes copied, which lowers the accountability of key locks.

Lock Picking
the art of opening a lock without a key.

Lock bumping
uses a shaved-down key which will physically fit into the lock. A shaved key is inserted into the lock and bumps the exposed portion sometimes with the handle of a screwdriver. This causes the pins to jump, and the attacker quickly turns the key and opens the lock.

Master Keys
The master key opens any lock for a given security zone in a building. Access to the master key should be tightly controlled, including the physical security of the key itself, authorization granted to a few critical employees, and accountability whenever the key is used.

Core key
The core key is used to remove the lock core in interchangeable core locks

Combination Locks
Combination locks have dials that must be turned to specific numbers, in a specific order to unlock.

Smart Card
A smart card is physical access control device which is often used for electronic locks, credit card purchases, or dual-factor authentication systems.

Smart cards
Smart cards may be "contact" or "contactless." Contact cards must be inserted into a smart card reader, while contactless cards are read wirelessly.

Radio-Frequency Identification RFID
contain RFID tags (also called transponders) which are read by RFID transceivers

Magnetic Stripe Cards

A magnetic stripe card contains a magnetic stripe which stores information. Unlike smart cards, magnetic stripe cards are passive devices that contain no circuits. These cards are sometimes called swipe cards: they are used by swiping through a card reader.

Tailgating/piggybacking

Tailgating also known as piggybacking occurs when an unauthorized person follows an authorized person into a building after the authorized person unlocks and opens the door.

Mantraps and Turnstiles

A mantrap is a preventive physical control with two doors. The first door must close and lock before the second door may be opened.

Turnstiles

Turnstiles are designed to prevent tailgating by enforcing a one person per authentication rule, just as they do in subway systems. Secure data centers often use floor-to-ceiling turnstiles with interlocking blades to prevent an attacker from going over or under the turnstile.

Contraband Checks

are often used to detect metals, weapons, or explosives. They may also be used to detect controlled substances such as illegal drugs. Another concern is portable cameras or storage media which may be used to exhilarate sensitive data.

Motion Detectors

A wave of energy is sent out, and the echo is returned when it

bounces off an object detecting the object

Photoelectric motion sensor
sends a beam of light across a monitored space to a photoelectric sensor. The sensor alerts when the light beam is broken.

magnetic door and window alarms
match pairs of sensors on the wall, as well as window/door. An electrical circuit flows through the sensor pairs as long as the door or window is closed; the circuit breaks when either is opened.

Door hinges
should face inward

Glass windows
are structurally weak and can be dangerous when shattered. Bullet-proof or explosive-resistant glass can be used for secured areas

Glass windows
Alternatives to glass windows include polycarbonate such as Lexan and acrylic such as Plexiglass.

Walls
Walls around any internal secure perimeter such as a data center should be slab to slab, meaning they should start at the floor slab, and run to the ceiling slab.

Walls
Any wall protecting a secure perimeter whether internal or external should be strong enough to resist cutting by an attacker attempting to create an ingress point.

Walls

Walls should have an appropriate fire rating. The fire resistant rating shall be commensurate with the exposure, but

not less than one hour.

Guards

Guards are a dynamic control which may be used in a variety of situations. Guards may aid in inspection of access credentials, monitor CCTVs, monitor environmental controls, respond to incidents, and serve as a deterrent

Guards

Criminals are more likely to target an unguarded building over a guarded building

Guards

Guard's orders should be complete and clear. Guards are often attacked via social engineering, so this threat should directly addressed via security awareness and training.

Dogs

Dogs provide perimeter defense

Dogs

Dogs primarily serve as both deterrent and detective controls. A site without dogs is more likely to be physically attacked than a site with dogs

Dogs

The primary drawback to using dogs as a perimeter control is legal liability.

SITE SELECTION, DESIGN, AND CONFIGURATION

Selection, Design, and Configuration describes the process of building a secure facility such as a data center, from the site selection process through the final design.

Topography

Topography is the physical shape of the land: hills, valleys, trees, etc. Highly secure sites such as military installations will leverage and sometimes alter the topography of the site as a defensive measure.

Topography

Topography can be used to steer ingress and egress to controlled points.

Utility Reliability

The reliability of local utilities is a critical concern for site selection purposes. Electrical outages are among the most common of all failures and disasters we experience.

Crime

Local crime rates also factor into site selection. The primary issue is employee safety: all employees have the right to a safe working environment. Additional issues include theft of company assets.

Site marking

Many data centers are not externally marked to avoid drawing attention to the facility. Similar controls include attention avoiding details such as muted building design.

Shared Tenancy

Other tenants in a building case pose security issues: they are already behind the physical security perimeter.

Shared Tenancy

Their physical security controls will impact yours: a tenant's poor visitor security practices can endanger your security

Adjacent buildings

Adjacent buildings pose a similar risk. Attackers can enter a less secure adjacent building and use that as a base to attack an adjacent building, often breaking in through a shared wall.

Shared Tenancy Adjacent buildings Wireless Security

Physical proximity is required to launch many types of wireless attacks. Also, neighbors running wireless equipment at the same frequency as you can cause interference, raising wireless availability issues.

Shared Demarc

A crucial issue to consider in a building with shared tenancy is a shared demarc the demarcation point, where the ISP's (Internet Service Provider responsibility ends and the customer's begins

Shared Demarc

Most buildings have one demarc area, where all external circuits enter the building. Access to the demarc allows attacks on the confidentiality, integrity, and availability of all circuits and the data flowing over them.

Shared Demarc

Shared demarcs should employ strong physical access control, including identifying, authenticating, and authorizing all access.

For very secure sites, construction of multiple segregated demarcs is recommended.

Asset Tracking
Detailed asset tracking databases enhance physical security.

Data such as serial numbers and model numbers are useful in cases of loss due to theft or disaster.

Port Controls
Port controls are critical because large amounts of information can be placed on a device small enough to evade perimeter contraband checks.

Port Controls
Ports may also be electronically locked via system policy. Locking ports via Microsoft Windows Active Directory Group Policy Object (GPO) is an example of enterprise-level port controls.

Drive and Tape Encryption
Drive and tape encryption protect data at rest, and are one of the few controls which will protect data after physical security has been breached.

Drive and Tape Encryption
Whole-disk encryption of mobile device hard drives is recommended.

Media Storage and Transportation
All sensitive backup data should be stored offsite, whether transmitted offsite via networks, or physically moved as backup media. Sites using backup media should follow strict procedures for rotating media offsite.

Media Storage and Transportation
Always use bonded and insured company for offsite media storage. The company should employ secure vehicles and store media at a secure site.

Media Storage and Transportation

Ensure that the storage site is unlikely to be impacted by the same disaster that may strike the primary site

Media Cleaning and Destruction

media should be securely cleaned or destroyed before disposal to prevent object reuse, which is the act of recovering information from previously used objects

Dumpster diving

searching for information by rummaging through unsecured trash

Media Cleaning and Destruction

All cleaning and destruction actions should follow a formal policy,

Media Cleaning and Destruction

all activity should be documented, including the serial numbers of any hard disks, type of data contained, date of cleaning or destruction, and personnel performing these actions.

Paper Shredders

Paper shredders cut paper to prevent object reuse

Paper Shredders

Cross-cut shredders are more secure than strip-cut, and cut both vertically and horizontally, creating small paper confetti

Paper Shredders

Given enough time and access to all of the shredded materials, attackers can recover shredded documents, though it is more difficult with cross-cut shredders.

Overwriting

Simply deleting a file removes the entry from the File Allocation Table (FAT) and marks the data blocks as "unallocated." Reformatting a disk destroys the old FAT and replaces it with a new one.

Degaussing and Destruction

Degaussing and destruction are controls used to prevent object reuse attacks against magnetic media such as magnetic tapes and disk drives.

Degaussing

Degaussing destroys the integrity of magnetic media such as tapes or disk drives by exposing them to a strong magnetic field, destroying the integrity of the media and the data it contains.

Destruction

Destruction physically destroys the integrity of magnetic media by damaging or destroying the media itself, such as the platters of a disk drive.

Destruction

Destructive measures include incineration, pulverizing, and bathing metal components in acid.

ENVIRONMENTAL CONTROLS

Environmental controls are designed to provide a safe environment for personnel and equipment. Power, HVAC, and fire safety are considered environmental controls.

Electricity

Reliable electricity is critical for any data center, and is one of the top priorities when selecting, building, and designing a site.

Types of Electrical Faults
• Blackout: prolonged loss of power

• Brownout: prolonged low voltage

• Fault: short loss of power

• Surge: prolonged high voltage

• Spike: temporary high voltage

• Sag: temporary low voltage

Surge Protectors
Surge Protectors protect equipment from damage due to electrical surges. They contain a circuit or fuse which is tripped during a power spike or surge, shorting the power or regulating it down to acceptable levels.

Uninterruptible Power Supplies
provide temporary backup power in the event of a power outage. They may also clean the power, protecting against surges, spikes, and other forms of electrical faults.

Generators
Generators are designed to provide power for longer periods of times than UPSs, and will run as long as fuel is available.

EMI
Network cables that are poorly shielded may suffer crosstalk, where magnetism from one cable crosses over to another nearby cable. This primarily impacts the integrity and may also affect the confidentiality of network or voice data.

HVAC

HVAC heating, ventilation, and air conditioning controls keep the air at a reason- able temperature and humidity. They operate in a closed loop, recirculating treated air. This helps reduce dust and other airborne contaminants.

Heat and Humidity

Data center HVAC units are designed to maintain optimum heat and humidity levels for computers. Humidity levels of 40-55% are recommended. A commonly recommended set point temperature range for a data center is 68-77 F 20-25 Celsius

Static

Static is mitigated by maintaining proper humidity, proper grounding all circuits in a proper manner, and using antistatic sprays, wrist straps, and work surfaces.

Corrosion

High humidity levels can allow the water in the air to condense onto and into equipment, which may lead to corrosion.

Airborne Contaminants

Dust is a common problem: airborne dust particles can be drawn into computer enclosures, where they become trapped. Built-up dust can cause overheating and static buildup.

Heat Detectors

Heat detectors alert when temperature exceeds an established safe baseline. They may trigger when a specific temperature is exceeded or when temperature changes at a specific rate such as 10 F in less than 5 minutes

Ionization-based smoke detectors

contain a small radioactive source which creates

a small electric charge.it alerts when smoke

interrupts the radioactivity or light

Photoelectric smoke detectors

use LED light. It alerts when the light is interrupted

Flame Detectors

Flame detectors detect infrared or ultraviolet light emitted in fire.

Flame Detectors

One drawback to this type of detection is that the detector usually requires line-of-site to detect the flame; smoke detectors do not have this limitation.

Evacuation Routes

Evacuation routes should be prominently posted, All personnel should be advised of the quickest evacuation route from their areas.

safety warden

The safety warden ensures that all personnel safely evacuate the building in the event of an emergency or drill.

meeting point leader

the meeting point leader assures that all personnel are

accounted for at the emergency meeting point

Class A fires

are common combustibles such as wood, paper, etc. This type of fire is the most common and should be extinguished with water or soda acid.

Class B fires

are burning alcohol, oil, and other petroleum products such as gasoline. They are extinguished with gas or soda acid. You should never use water to extinguish a class B fire.

Class C fires

are electrical fires which are fed by electricity and may occur in

equipment or wiring. Electrical fires are Conductive fires, and the extinguishing

agent must be non-Conductive, such as any type of gas.

Class C fires

Many sources erroneously list soda acid as recommended for class C fires: this is incorrect, as soda acid can conduct electricity.

Class D fires

are burning metals and are extinguished with dry powder.

Class K fires

are kitchen fires, such as burning oil or grease. Wet chemicals are used to extinguish class K fires.

Backup and Archive

What is a Backup?
- additional copy of production data that is created and retained for the sole purpose of recovering lost or corrupted data

Backups are performed to serve three purposes:
- Disaster recovery

- Operational recovery

- archive

Backup Granularity
-Full Backup

-Incremental Backup

- Cumulative (Differential) Backup

Full Backup
-backup of complete data on the production volumes

Incremental Backup
- copies the data that has changed since the last full or incremental backup, whichever has occurred more recently

Cumulative Backup
- copies the data that has changed since the last full backup

Restoring from Incremental Backup

- less # of files to be back up, less time to backup and requires less storage space

- longer restore because last full and all subsequent incremental backups must be applied

Restoring from Cumulative Backup
- more files to be backed up, more time to back up and requires more storage

- faster restore because only last full and last cumulative must be applied

Backup Architecture
- Backup client

- backup server

- storage node

Backup Client
- Gathers the data that is to be backed up and send it to the storage node

Backup Server
- manages backup operations and maintains backup catalog

Storage Node
- responsible for writing data to backup device

- manages the backup device

Backup Operation

1. Backup server initiates scheduled backup

2. Backup server retrieves backup related info from backup catalog

3. Backup server instructs storage node to load media to backup device and instructs backup clients to send data to be backed up to storage node

4. Backup clients send data to storage node and update backup catalog on backup server

5. storage node sends data to backup device

6. storage node sends metadata and media info to backup server

7. Backup server updates catalog

Recovery Operation
1. Backup client request backup server for data restore

2. Backup server scans catalog to identify data to be restored and client which will receive data

3. Backup server instructs storage node to load backup media to device

4. Data is then read and sent to backup client

5. Storage node sends restore metadata to backup server

6. Backup server updates catalog

Backup Methods
- Hot or online (application is up and running, open file agent can be used to backup open files)

- Cold or Offline (requires application to be shutdown during the backup process)

Bare metal recovery
- OS, hardware, and App configs are appropriately backed up for a full system recovery

- Server config backup (SCB) can also recover server into dissimilar hardware

Server Configuration Backup (SCB)
- creates and backs up server config profiles, based on user define schedule

- profiles used to config the recovery server in case of production failure

2 types of profiles used:

- base profile: contains key elements of the OS required to recover server

-extended: typically larger than base profile& contains all necessary info to rebuild app environment

Backup Topologies
- Direct Attached Backup

- LAN Based Backup

- SAN based backup

- Mixed backup topology

Direct Attached Backup
- storage node is configured on a backup client and backup device is directly attached to client

LAN based backup

- clients, backup server, storage node, and backup device are connected to LAN

- data transferred via LAN, affects network performance

SAN Based Backup

-aka LAN free backup

- backup device and clients are attached to SAN

- backup data traffic is restricted to SAN, only metadata is transported across LAN

Common Backup Implementations in a NAS environment

- Server-based backup

- Serverless backup

- NDMP 2 way backup

- NDMP 3 way backup

Server Based Backup

NAH head retrieves data from a storage array over the network and transfers it to the backup client running on the application server

result is overload the network with backup data and using app server resources to move the backup data

Serverless Backup

- network share is mounted directly on the storage node

- avoids overloading the network and eliminates use of resources from application server

NDMP 2 way
- NDMP (industry based TCP/IP protocol designed for backup in NAS environment

- network traffic is minimized by isolating data movement from the NAS head to the locally attached backup device

-only metadata is transported on the network

NAS acts as a client and storage node

NDMP 3 way
- separate private backup network(private LAN) must be established between all NAS heads and NAS head connected to the backup device

metadata and ndmp control data transferred across public network

Backup to Tape
- low cost

- sequential/linear access

- limitations of tape include:

--backup and recovery are slow due to sequential access

--wear and tear of tape

--shipping/handling challenges

--controlled environment required for tape storage

--"shoe shinning effect" or "backhitching"

Shoe Shinning effect or "Backhitching"
-repeated back and forth motion a tape drive makes when there is an interruption in the backup data stream

- causes degradation of service and excessive wear and tear to tapes

Backup to disk
- enhanced overall backup and recovery performance

-random access

multiple host access simultaneously

Backup to Virtual Tape
- disks are emulated and presented as tapes to backup software

- does not require any additional modules or changes in the legacy backup software

- provides better single stream performance and reliability over physical tape

-online and random disk access

Virtual Tape Library
-VTL use disks as backup media. Emulation software has a database with a list of virtual tapes, and teach VT is assigned space on a LUN. VT can space multiple LUNs if requires.
-

Data Deduplication
- process of identifying and eliminating redundant data

Deduplication Methods
- File level: single instance storage

detects and removed redundant copies of identical files. after a file is stored, all other references to the same file refer to original copy

- subfile level

detects redundant data within and across files

two methods: fixed length block and variable length segment

Deduplication Technologies
- source based: EMC Avamar

- target based: Data Domain

Source Based Data Deduplication
- Avamar

- data deduplicated at source (backup client)

-reduced storage capacity and network bandwidth requirements

-increased overhead on the backup client

Target Based Data Deduplication

- Data Domain

- data deduplicated at the target (inline and post process)

-offloads the backup client from deduplication process

-all data travels across network

Data Deduplication Benefits
- reduces infrastructure costs

- enables longer retention periods

- reduces backup window

-reduces backup bandwidth requirement

Virtual Environment Backup Approach
-Backup agent on VM

- Backup agent on hypervisor

- image based backup

Backup agent on VM
- requires agent on each vm

-only backs up virtual disk data

- does not capture swap file or config file

Backup agent on hypervisor
-agent only on hypervisor

-backs up all vm files

Image Based backup
- creates a copy of the guest OS, vm state, and configs

- mounts image on a proxy server

-offloads processing from hypervisor

Data Archive
repository where fix content is stored

-archives implemented as: online, nearline, offline

Online: immediately accessible

nearline; device must be mounted

offline: manual intervention is required

CAS (Content Addressed Storage)
disk based online accessibility to archive data

object based storage

features

- content authenticity and content integrity

- location independence

- single instance storage

- retention enforcement

- data protection

Services

Extensible Markup Language (XML)
a language based on the same principles as HTML, with the added ability to create custom tags

extranet
a network that allows external and internal access to web pages by authorized personnel

HTML tag
an instruction for how text and graphics should appear when displayed in a web browser

Hypertext Markup Language (HTML)
a programming language used to create web pages

Hypertext Transport Protocol
a protocol designed for communications between a web browser and a web server

Internet
a collection of interconnected networks from all around the world

Internet Message Access Protocol (IMAP)

a mail access protocol that can manipulate data while it is on the server. Also allows user to access mail while leaving a copy on the server.

intranet
private network that provides web page distribution to a specific group of users within a LAN

mail filter
blocks unwanted email messages

mail gateway
a software/computer combination used to connect two otherwise incompatible email systems

Multipurpose Internet Mail Extensions (MIME)
a protocol that encodes additional information known as mail attachments to email protocols that normally would not transfer attachments such as graphics

Network News Transfer Protocol (NNTP)
TCP/IP protocol designed to distribute news messages to NNTP servers and NNTP clients across the Internet

newsgroup
news articles that are arranged in a group or category on an NNTP server.

Post Office Protocol (POP)
mail access protocol designed to access a mail server and download messages to the email client

Secure File Transfer Protocol (SFTP)
encrypts the user name, password, and data during a file transfer session

Simple Mail Transfer Protocol (SMTP)
TCP/IP protocol designed to transfer plain text email messages from email clients to email servers as well as between email servers

Simple Object Access Protocol (SOAP)
XML message format that allows a client to freely interact with a web page on the web server, rather than download it

Soapy Hands Are Major Protocol-Oriented Objects (SHAMPOO)
What you wash your hair with

spam
unwanted email such as advertisements

spammer
someone who engages in distributing unsolicited email or sending email with some sort of advertisement as a probe

Trivial File Transport Protocol (TFTP)
file transfer that does not require a user name or password because it uses UDP packets for transferring data

Uniform Resource Locator (URL)
a user-friendly name that allows users access to web-based resources

web browser

program that allows user to navigate the World Wide Web and displays and interprets web pages

web server

a server configured to provide, such as web pages, file transfer, and HTML-based email

web site

a location on the World Wide Web that contains a collection of related web pages and files

application servers

catalog display

provides a database for product description and prices

transaction processing

shopping cart; accepts orders and clears payments

list server

creates and serves mailing lists and manages e-mail marketing campaigns

proxy server

monitors and controls access to main web server; firewall protection

mail server

manages internet e-mail

audio/video server
stores and delivers streaming media content

chat server
creates an environment for online real-time text and audio transactions

news server
provides connectivity and displays internet news feeds

fax server
provides fax reception and sending using a web server

groupware server
creates group work environments for online collaboration

database server
stores customer, product, and price information

auction server
provides a transaction environment for conducting online auctions

B2B server
implements buy, sell, and link marketplaces for commercial transactions

ad server
maintains Web-enabled database of advertising banners that permits customized and personalized display of advertisements based on consumer behavior and characteristics

Server Basics

File and Print Servers

File servers are network servers that store data files and programs. A file server is

basically a remote disk drive that is shared by the network users.

File servers are not the

same as application servers: An application server runs programs and processes data; a file server stores files and programs. A file server can be any computer that shares a file, folder or entire disk drive with the network. It should be a powerful server capable of high speeds, security and data protection.

Network printers allow multiple users to send print jobs to the same physical printers. Without network printing capability, any user who wanted to print would need a printer physically attached to his or her computer, or would need to copy the document to a computer that had a printer attached. Because this arrangement would become cost-prohibitive in even small offices, most LANs use network-printing functions.

The Linux/UNIX network operating system can use the Line printer/line printer daemon (LPR/LPD) printing protocol to

submit print jobs to network printers. When a user submits a file for printing, the file is

transmitted over the network in one direction (unidirectional). The LPR initiates commands and the LPD executes them. The commands manage the submission of print jobs to the printer, such as print queue management, and the transfer of print jobs from the print queue to the printer.

HTTP Server Essentials

The World Wide Web is a collection of computer systems running the HTTP service.

(Remember that HTTP, on which the Web operates, is a TCP/IP application-layer protocol.) These computer systems (servers) act together as document delivery systems.

Documents are delivered to systems running Web browsers (also called clients) as well as

to user agents. These client systems request documents from HTTP servers, which are

usually called Web servers. The documents that the server processes may be from a disk

archive, or they may be created dynamically when the client requests them. The HTTP

server and the Web browser are examples of client/server communications. A Web browser is a software application that interprets and displays HTML documents.

Worldwide interaction between the HTTP server and the Web browser also exemplifies the

hyper-distributed networking involved in Web-based networking. A Web site is a collection of documents and applications that create documents. The site

is organized around a Web server process, which runs as a daemon process on

Linux/UNIX systems and as a service on Windows systems. The Web server process

binds to TCP Port 80 by default and listens for incoming requests from clients such as

Web browsers. These requests are formed in a language called Hypertext Markup Language (HTML). The applications used by Web servers to create documents dynamically are called Common Gateway Interface (CGI) applications (or scripts).

Web server role
The HTTP (i.e., Web) server has access to a set of documents that it may return to a client

in response to an appropriate request. These documents are located in a mass storage

device, such as a hard drive, in a specific location that the server can read. These

documents can be in a wide range of formats. For example, the server probably has

access to a large collection of HTML documents as well as the associated image files in a

range of formats. In addition, the server may be able to supply many other multimedia

documents, such as sound files and video clips.

HTTP servers and MIME
An HTTP server can download any file type. Although a Web browser renders only certain

types of images, HTTP can process a variety of file types. The Multipurpose Internet

Mail Extensions (MIME) system allows HTTP and e-mail attachments to identify the files

they must use. A version of MIME that encrypts MIME data, called Secure MIME (S/MIME), is used for secure transmissions.

Whenever data is passed between a Web server and a browser, the data is labeled with its MIME type. The recipient uses the MIME type to render the information.

MIME type
Identifies the contents of a file in

the MIME encoding system using a type/subtype

format; examples are image/jpg and text/plain.

HTTP servers and the operating system
HTTP servers work closely with the computer's operating system. One way to describe

their interaction is that an HTTP server resides "on top of" the other services that form

the operating system.

Server security and operating system security
Most Web servers can restrict files, folders and directories by establishing permissions.

Permissions include the ability to read a file (read permission), create or delete a file

(write permission), execute programs (execute permission) or deny access (no access).

Operating systems can also establish permissions.

Access control

An important part of setting up and managing a Web server (or any other server type) is

access control, which is similar to permissions. Most Web sites offer access to the general

public; users do not need special permission to access such server resources. This type of access is often called anonymous access. However, some sites need to restrict access to some or all of their server resources. An

Access Control List (ACL) defines the permissions for a resource by specifying which

users and groups have access to the resource.

The traditional method of restricting access to server resources is based on a

database of permitted users, who must supply a password to access particular server

information. The database of permitted users may be:

Users with accounts on the host system.

A special database managed by the server itself.

The second method separates people with permission to access Web server information

from those with more global permission on the host system. Because thousands of users

may be allowed to access information, the second method is much better for restricting

access.

The access control restrictions discussed previously are enforced in the following two

stages:

1. The Web server process checks to see whether certain actions are allowed, based on

its configuration information.

2. The operating system enforces restrictions on actions that the Web server process

can perform.

The operating system restrictions are based on the fact that the Web server process is owned by a user account on the host computer, and is subject to limitations imposed on that account. In general, the

restrictions imposed by the operating system are more reliable than those imposed by the Web server alone.

Aliases and virtual directories

As part of their configuration options, most Web servers allow flexible mapping of URL

path names to file names. This kind of mapping has various names, including virtual

directories and aliases. Some of the advantages of flexible mapping of URL path names to

file names include the following examples:

The more flexible the mapping from URL path names to file names, the more freedom the administrator has to arrange files on the disk.

If a set of documents may be reasonably accessed under several URL path names, all

these URL path names can be mapped to the same file names.

Logging

The following three types of information are usually collected in server logs:

Access data — Each time a client issues an HTTP command to the server, the command is logged.

Referrer data — Part of the information transmitted by a browser to a server is the

URL at which the browser is pointing when it makes the request. This information

may be logged to indicate how users enter the site.

Error data — Server errors (including improperly formatted HTTP requests, dropped

TCP connections and access violations) are logged to help monitor server operations.

Monitoring server and network bandwidth use

Monitoring server and network bandwidth use is key to maintaining consistent

performance. It allows network administrators to identify network bottlenecks in a timely

manner. Bottlenecks usually occur when a server or network is flooded with traffic and

cannot perform at acceptable levels.

A baseline is a recording of network activity, obtained through documentation and monitoring, that serves as an example for comparing future network activity. Baselines

should be recorded when a network is running correctly. If problems are introduced to

the network, the new network behavior can be compared with the baseline. Baselines can

be used to determine bottlenecks, identify heavy traffic patterns, and analyze daily

network use and protocol patterns.

The Windows Vista Reliability And Performance Monitor can determine a baseline for the

number of packets per second sent to a system over a network.

During peak network traffic periods, or when performance is noticeably slower, Reliability

And Performance Monitor can be used to collect data and compare it with the baseline. If

the new data shows a significant increase in network traffic, processor or memory use, changes may be required. For instance, you may need to install a faster processor or more RAM on the server. You may need to increase your network bandwidth by upgrading the network from Ethernet to Fast Ethernet, or replace a problem hub with a switch.

Common Web servers
The most common Web servers include:

Apache server (www.apache.org)

Microsoft Internet information Services (IIS) (www.microsoft.com)

Sun Java System Web Server (www.sun.com).

Server-side technologies

Web servers often run programs to help enhance a Web page or provide access to database servers. These programs are called server-side applications. Examples of serverside

technologies include:

JavaServer Pages (JSP) — Sun's solution. You can learn more about JSP at

www.sun.com.

Active Server Pages (ASP) and .NET — Microsoft's server-side scripting solutions.

ASP is an older solution. You can learn more about ASP and .NET at www.microsoft.com.

PHP Hypertext Preprocessor (PHP) — An open-source solution. You can learn more

about PHP at www.php.net.

Each of these languages can be used to implement CGI.

Open Database Connectivity (ODBC)

ODBC is a standard developed by Microsoft that allows databases created by various vendors to communicate with one another. ODBC is often used with server-side languages. It is also used by database servers. When creating an entry in ODBC, you need to register the database in ODBC and provide a data source name (DSN), which contains all the necessary connectivity information. Specific information you need to provide includes the vendor's database driver, the name of the database, a user ID and the location of the database. Several types of DSN exist. The most common are the system DSN, which all users can employ, and a user DSN, which is designed for use only by a specific user.

Database Servers

A database is a file that stores information in a series of tables and columns. Tables in a

database contain fields that allow data to be read and cross-referenced. Many different types of databases exist, including flat file databases (for example, the Windows registry) and relational databases. A relational database allows you to

manipulate information contained in tables and columns. All database servers present relational databases, and make it possible for remote individuals (for example, users with Web browsers) and hosts (for example, Web servers) to access the data. A database server can be installed on a dedicated system or on the same system as a Web server. In either case, a Web server is often configured to present HTML/XHTML pages that present

information obtained from a relational database.

Database servers and Structured Query Language (SQL)

All database servers use Structured Query Language (SQL) to create, maintain and
query databases. Commands such as SELECT, FROM and JOIN can be used to create,

maintain and manipulate tables. Often, a Web site administrator will need to use SQL to ensure that a Web page presents valid database information on a page.

Proxy Servers

A proxy server is an intermediary between a network host and other hosts outside the

network. Its main functions are to provide enhanced security, manage TCP/IP addresses

and speed access to the Internet by providing caching server functions for frequently

used documents.

In a network setting, a proxy server replaces the network IP address with another,

contingent address. This process effectively hides the actual IP address from the rest of the Internet, thereby protecting the entire network.

Proxy servers can provide the following additional services:

Caching of Web documents -

If corporate users access information on a Web server

from the Internet, that information is cached to the local proxy server. This caching

allows anyone on the corporate intranet to access the same information from the local system instead of repeatedly downloading the files from the Internet. This feature reduces the amount of network traffic produced on the Internet, which leads to improved performance for the corporate intranet and the Internet.

Corporate firewall access — A proxy server can provide safe passage for corporate users to the Internet through a firewall, allowing protected use of HTTP and FTP.

Filtering client transactions — A proxy can control access to remote Web servers and their resources by filtering client transactions. Filtering is accomplished by limiting or denying access to specific URLs, specific host IP addresses, domain names, host or computer names, Web contents, and specific users.

Transaction logging — Proxy servers generally support transaction logging. Network

administrators can track client activity and customize which data to record. Some of the data that can be logged includes accessed URLs, dates and times, and the byte counts of all data that has been transferred. Information on routing and success of a transaction can also be logged and used to evaluate network performance.

Securing internal hosts — A proxy server can help isolate internal systems so that they cannot be as easily attacked from systems based on the Internet.

Proxy server configuration

If your network uses a proxy server, you must ensure that all the clients are properly

configured. You must configure every application to work with your proxy server, including Web browsers, Telnet applications and FTP programs. Otherwise, not all applications will be able to access outside networks.

Mail Servers

A mail server stores and/or forwards e-mail messages using several protocols, including

SMTP, POP3 and IMAP. Simple Mail Transfer Protocol (SMTP) is responsible solely for sending e-mail messages.

In Linux/UNIX, the send mail program activates in response to a command and sends the

requested message.

Two methods are used to store and access e-mail messages:

Post Office Protocol version 3 (POP3) — POP3 servers store and forward e-mail messages to the host.

Internet Message Access Protocol (IMAP) — IMAP handles messages in a more sophisticated manner because it allows a user to browse and manage files remotely, whereas a POP3 server forces a user to download files before reading, deleting or otherwise managing them.

Mail servers and MIME

MIME is commonly used to transmit files with e-mail. MIME identifies a file type, encodes the file and decodes it at the receiving end so it will display properly. MIME performs these steps by adding a header to each file. The MIME header contains the encoding method and the type of data contained within. The different MIME types are classified under broad headings (text, image, application, audio and video), and then sub classified by exact type. E-mail typically uses MIME for non-text file transfers.

Whenever data is passed between an e-mail sender and recipient, the data is labeled with

its MIME type. The recipient uses the MIME type to render the information. The same

procedure is used by a Web server to transmit files to browser clients.

Problems with mail servers

Mail servers can experience various problems, including the following:

A virus or worm attack, in which a program replicates itself on the computer system,

usually through executable software, and causes system damage. A slowdown in which the e-mail server may be running low on RAM or disk space. Sometimes, however, problems with other network devices can slow e-mail. For example, if you experience slow e-mail, a firewall or other intermediate device may be creating a bottleneck.

Instant Messaging (IM)

Instant messaging (IM) is a computer-based method of communication that allows

individuals to communicate in real time. It is usually a service that runs on a typical server installation (e.g., Microsoft Windows or Linux). You can use IM to type and view messages sent to one or more recipients, and view the responses immediately. Unlike email,

which can be sent whether your recipient is online or not, instant messages can be sent only to contacts who are currently online — that is, logged on to an IM service.

A central IM server controls access, and allows you to specify individuals with whom you want to communicate. To use IM, you must install a client on your system and then

register for service.

Multi-protocol IM clients

Each IM service provides client software for you to use. However, you are not limited to

using these. You can use third-party software that supports multiple IM protocols.

For example, Pidgin is a multi-protocol instant messaging client for Linux, BSD,

Mac OS X and Windows. It is compatible with AIM, ICQ, Windows Live Messenger,

Yahoo!, Internet Relay Chat (IRC), Jabber, Gadu-Gadu and Zephyr networks. Pidgin

allows you to perform IM with users at various other networks (such as AOL, Yahoo! and

MSN) simultaneously. You can download Pidgin at www.pidgin.im/. Trillian

(www.trillian.im) is another example of a multi-protocol IM client.

Mailing List Servers

A mailing list server is a standard SMTP server that can automatically forward an e-mail

message to every member on a distribution list. Some mailing list servers, such as

LISTSERV (www.listserv.net or www.lsoft.com), are designed for this purpose. Other

SMTP servers, such as Microsoft Exchange Server, can be configured as mailing list

servers.

A mailing list server allows people to work together even though their e-mail accounts

reside on different e-mail servers across the Internet.

In effect, a mailing list server allows you to imitate a newsgroup. The main difference is that any e-mail message you send does not remain persistent on a central server for a

given time. The interface that allows you to configure a mailing list server is often called a Mailing List Manager (MLM). Using an MLM, you can customize the behavior of the mailing list server.

Public and private mailing lists

You can create public or private mailing lists with a mailing list server. Examples of public mailing lists include the well-known LISTSERV and Majordomo groups. You can configure a public mailing

list server to allow anyone to join the list at any time.

The specific syntax and information requirements differ from one public mailing list

server to another. Most servers allow users to join a mailing list automatically by having them send an e-mail message with the word "join" or "subscribe" in the body of the message or the header. Users can unsubscribe from a mailing list by sending an e-mail message with words such as "unsubscribe" or "remove" in the message or header.

Media Servers

A media server offers streaming audio and video over a network. This type of server is suited for intranets as well as the Internet. More popular vendors include Microsoft Windows Media Services (www.microsoft.com/windows/windowsmedia/) and RealPlayer

(www.real.com).

These servers are useful because businesses and other organizations use the Internet to

conduct long-distance conference calls as personally as possible. Generally, these servers use UDP ports and buffers to achieve the effect of a real-time connection.

DNS Servers

Invented by Paul Mockapetris in 1984, the Domain Name System (DNS) is a mechanism used on the Internet to translate host computer names into IP addresses. Without DNS, users would be forced to enter long numerical strings every time they needed access to any part of the Internet.

DNS servers, also called name servers, contain the server application that supports

name-to-address translation.

Typically, the system on which the name server resides is called the name server system.

Hosts file

Until DNS was implemented, a single file known as the hosts table was managed and

updated by the Stanford Research Institute Network Information Center (SRI-NIC).

Whenever network administrators needed the latest hosts table for their name servers, they downloaded it from the SRI-NIC FTP server. As the Internet grew, this file became very large and difficult to manage, and no longer provided an effective way to distribute name-to-address data.

The hosts file on your computer (which you were introduced to earlier in the course) is

similar to the hosts table used earlier for the Internet. The hosts file is a simple text file

that is referenced locally by applications and commands for name-to-address resolution.

DNS hierarchy

DNS is hierarchical and distributed. It consists of three levels — root-level, top-level and

second-level domains — and is often referred to as the domain name space.

The root-level domain is the top of the hierarchy. It contains entries for each top-level

domain. The root-level domain is updated daily and replicated on root domain servers

across the Internet. It is expressed by a period (.). This period is usually removed from the end of domain names (for example, www.company.com instead of www.company.com.).

The top-level domain is one level below the root-level domain. It consists of categories

found at the end of domain names (such as .com or .uk). It divides domains into

organizations (.org), businesses (.com), countries (.uk) and other categories. Each top-level

domain has a master server that contains entries for all registered second-level

domains (such as company.com).

The first seven domains are associated with the United States and are assigned by the Internet Network Information Center (InterNIC). However, the majority of top-level domains are country codes. Each country assigns domain names using its own standards. The third type of

top-level Internet domains (shown in Table 3-3) is designated by category; these domains were recently approved by the ICANN.

The second-level domain is one level below the top-level domain. Second-level domains

include the businesses and institutions that register their domain names with the top-level

domains (through their respective registrars).

Second-level domains include registered names such as the following:

 iso.ch

 amazon.com

Second-level domains can also be categories of top-level domains. For example, the

United States domain (us) is further categorized into a second-level domain for each

state, such as California:

ca.us

Companies and academic institutions in the United Kingdom (and most other countries) are also categorized, as shown:

co.uk

ac.uk

Finally, second-level domains can be divided into subdomains. For example, a subdomain of the second-level domain company.com may be as follows:

sales.company.com

DNS components
DNS consists of the following two key components:

Name server — a server that supports name-to-address translation and runs the

DNS service.

Name resolver — software that uses the services of one or more name servers to resolve unknown requests. For example, if a host requests www.novell.com, and the DNS server does not have the name information, it will use name resolver software to ask another name server on the DNS hierarchy. DNS clients and servers use name resolver software.

DNS server types
The following server types are included in the DNS model:

Root server — Root servers can identify all top-level domains on the Internet. If a client requests information about a host in another domain, any server (except a secondary server, which will be introduced shortly) can communicate that request to the root server. Most server administrators will never configure a root server.

Primary server — A primary server is the authority for a domain and maintains the DNS databases for its domain. It is the first DNS server in a domain. Companies and ISPs that implement their own DNS and participate on the Internet require a primary server. Primary servers are also called master servers.

Secondary server — A secondary server receives its authority and database from the

primary server. Secondary servers are used by server administrators to provide fault

tolerance, load distribution and easier remote name resolution for the primary DNS server. Secondary servers are also called slave servers.

Caching-only server — A caching-only server is one that does not contain its own zone file, but receives entries from other DNS servers.

zone file - A file containing a

set of instructions for

resolving a specific domain name into its numerical IP

address. Found in DNS servers.

Forwarding server — A forwarding server is one that receives requests and then

forwards them to other servers.

Linux/UNIX BIND servers are the most widely used DNS servers on the Internet.

DNS records

Every domain consists of DNS records. A DNS record is an entry in a DNS database (on a primary server) that provides additional routing and resolution information.

Common DNS records:

Name Server (NS) - Identifies DNS servers for the DNS domain.

Start Of Authority (SOA) - Identifies the DNS server that is the best source of information for the DNS domain. Because several backup DNS servers may exist, this record identifies the primary server for the specified DNS domain.

Address (A) - The most commonly used record; associates a host to an IP address. For example, you can establish an association between an IP address and a Web server by creating an address record.

Canonical Name (CNAME) - Creates an alias for a specified host. For example, the name of a

WWW server is server1.company.com (Web servers are commonly

named WWW). A CNAME record creates a "WWW" alias to the

server1.company.com host so it can also be accessed at

www.company.com.

Mail Exchanger (MX) - Identifies a server used to process and deliver e-mail messages for

the domain.

DNS process example
You work at company XYZ with the domain name xyz.com. You send an e-mail message

to a person at the International Organization for Standardization (ISO), which has the domain name iso.ch. Before your computer sends the message, it needs the IP address of the iso.ch mail server. Following are the steps taken in this process:

1. Your computer sends a DNS request to your configured name server.

2. Your name server queries itself for the requested entry. If an entry does not exist in

its cache, it will forward the request to the Internet's root servers.

3. A root server will send your name server the reference information for the requested

domain's (iso.ch) primary and secondary name servers.

4. Your name server will query the iso.ch primary (or secondary) name server for the

requested record. The request will be fulfilled with the iso.ch name server sending the

requested IP address.

5. Your name server will provide your computer with your request's IP address.

The lookup command

The nslookup command can be used to query Internet domain name servers to learn

name-to-IP-address mappings. This command is used for any system (for example, a

workstation or a server). The user has the option to request a specific name server to provide information about a given host or to get a list of all hosts in a given domain. The nslookup command is usually used at a command prompt or a Linux/UNIX terminal. By default, the nslookup command will query the default DNS server used by the system you

are using.

You can use nslookup as a one-time command or as an interactive command. When used as a one-time command, it will return information for only one system or zone.

Following is the syntax for using nslookup as a one-time command:

nslookup options address

Following is an example of a one-time use of nslookup:

nslookup www.CIWcertified.com

You can also use nslookup interactively. You will then be placed into an nslookup session, which allows you to make queries for multiple systems. You can also use an interactive session to list the contents of entire zones (if allowed), and to switch from your default DNS server to another DNS server (if allowed). Your command prompt or terminal will change from a standard prompt to the >

(greater than) character. You can then issue commands to determine name resolution.

To obtain a list of all nodes in a given domain, such as CIWcertified.com, execute the

following sequence of commands:

nslookup

> ls CIWcertified.com

You must have permission to list the domain with the DNS administrator. If not, you will

receive an error that says: "***Can't list domain: Bad error value."

FTP Servers
Most of the Internet server suites include an FTP server.

In most situations, if you have a file approaching 2 megabytes (MB), you should transfer it by means of FTP, because sending such a large file through a mail server slows that server and the network. In addition, if the mail server has difficulty transferring a large file, it will no longer forward that message. However, it will not delete the message; the message will remain in the e-mail server queue until a server administrator deletes it.

With FTP, on the other hand, if a problem occurs with the file, you need only resend it.

Thus, little administrative intervention is needed. Also, e-mail servers will often silently drop e-mail attachments of various types. This fact

alone makes e-mail servers inefficient methods for transferring and storing many files.

Logging and access control
FTP servers log all traffic (which is usually anonymous). You can consult the FTP server logs to determine the amount of traffic.

News Servers
News servers use the Network News Transfer Protocol (NNTP). Like the standard office bulletin board, a news server allows users to post information in an easily accessible location. Using a news server, you can secure specific

newsgroups, or (as in the case of the popular Usenet newsgroups) you can leave them open to the public. One of the most important uses for a newsgroup is to provide a forum for groups to communicate while developing projects.

To read a newsgroup, the user opens a news reader software program, such as that found

in Microsoft Outlook Express or the Mozilla Thunderbird newsgroup news client. The

news client locates the news server containing the newsgroup and requests access. After access is granted, the client can access the newsgroups on the news server.

When one newsgroup server communicates with another to gain access to the central

newsgroup files, the action is called a newsfeed.

Newsgroup security

Many administrators use news servers to create secure newsgroups. You can achieve

security by enabling user-specific password protection, or by means of a Secure Sockets

Layer (SSL) session. Although both of these solutions are secure, an SSL session

provides greater security. To enable an SSL session, you need to obtain a certificate that

enables encryption. You can obtain a certificate from a company such as VeriSign, or configure and use a certificate server.

Secure Sockets Layer (SSL) - A protocol that provides

authentication and encryption, used by most servers for

secure exchanges over the Internet. Superseded by

Transport Layer Security (TLS).

Certificate Servers

Certificate servers validate, or certify, keys. Keys are strings of text generated from a complex series of encryption algorithms that allow you to secure communication for a company or group of users. Many Web servers, such as IIS, create keys that, after having been validated, can be applied to other servers, such as news servers, mail servers or

Web servers. The purpose of this process is to create a way for people to communicate

and be reasonably sure that others are not eavesdropping or assuming a false identity.

The nature of e-mail and newsgroup servers and protocols makes them susceptible to identity theft. Digital certificates help minimize this security risk by authenticating users before they transmit information. A digital certificate is a password-protected, encrypted data file containing message encryption, user identification and message text. It is used to authenticate a program or a sender's public key, or to initiate SSL sessions. It must be signed by a certificate authority (CA) to be valid.

Directory Servers

A directory server is a dedicated server that identifies all resources on a network. It

makes these resources available to authenticated users.

A directory server allows users to remotely access such information quickly from a central location because it allows them to query the database without affecting

network performance. An administrator need only configure employee e-mail programs to query the database.

Additional directory service uses

A directory service enables a company to reuse the information in its directory, keep

management costs from increasing, and avoid re-entry of user information for every

application that requires such information. A directory service can also help administrators manage applications and users, and can help users locate other users or e-mail addresses.

In addition, a directory service can help with the following procedures:

Locating and managing all company accounts with the same directory.

Allowing users, both inside and outside the network, to use the service. For example, an office in one city can store the directory information about all its members on one server. Users outside that office can also access the information, with permission.

Maintaining a single database of e-mail contacts.

Directory service protocols

1. X.500 is used to manage user and resource directories. It is based on a hierarchical system that can classify entries by country, state, city and street, for example. The X.500

protocol was designed to offer a global directory. It has had limited success on its own

because it is complex and difficult to implement, but it has been the basis for many other

directory services.

X.500 directories offer the following characteristics:

Scalability — can be offered as a global database, but can also be divided into smaller databases for efficient management.

Synchronization — can synchronize with other directories to ensure all data is

current.

Replication — can replicate with other X.500 directories, thereby making all database copies identical (for reducing retrieval time) and creating backup copies.

2. LDAP was developed from X.500 at the University of Michigan. It is easier to implement than X.500 because it is based on TCP/IP, allowing communication on intranets as well as the Internet. LDAP uses a simplified X.500 directory structure and a simplified

directory-access method.

Fax Servers

A fax server is an alternative to providing individual fax machines throughout a company location. A fax server provides a centrally located fax system for all company departments, and can save costs from purchasing dozens of individual fax machines. Fax servers consist of a bank of fax modems. These modems allow outgoing and incoming faxes to be processed by the next available fax modem. Because fax services do not consume large amounts of network resources, a fax service is

often installed on a server running another service. For instance, fax services are often

installed on company file servers.

Transaction Servers

When a transaction takes place, such as ordering office supplies over the Internet with a company credit card, a transaction server guarantees that all required databases are

updated. It verifies that all parts of a transaction have taken place successfully. In some

cases, this task is complicated. For example, the online merchant's database must reflect the transaction, as well as the credit card company's and, in some cases, the

manufacturer's database.

Transaction servers are intended as client/server replacements for Customer Information Control System (CICS) mainframe servers. Transaction servers are Web-based and allow a network to provide a stand-alone solution or a bridging tool to mainframe servers.

A transaction server also comes preconfigured to connect to databases, thereby enabling the spontaneous transfer of information. Specifically built to enable a three-tier solution,

transaction servers allow high-volume transactions with minimal network overhead.

Choosing Web Server Products

As a networking professional, you will need to make and justify decisions. Part of this

decision-making process is learning what a company truly requires and then making the

appropriate choices.

Descriptions of some industry-standard Internet servers.

Apache Web server:

A tested, well-accepted solution. It is considered extremely reliable. As of this writing, almost half of all Web sites deliver their information with this server. The Apache Web server is part of the open-source movement (provides free source code to the development community at large with the goal of developing better products; includes Apache Web server and Linux.

Microsoft Internet Information Services (IIS):

One of the strengths of IIS is that it allows you to use a remote server to store and

retrieve files. The remote server need not be a Web server itself, a fact that allows you to

distribute the processing load evenly.

Sun Java System Web Server:

The Sun Java System Web Server supports JavaServer Pages (JSP) technology and Java servlets. These interpreters allow you to use Java to connect to databases; in addition, you can implement other server-side scripting applications.

Java software and Web servers:

Many Web servers use Java. Any time Java code is compiled and run solely on the Web

server, it is known as a servlet. A Java servlet is an application that resides on a server.

These applications can provide various services, including database connectivity. Servlets

allow the following:

Chaining, which allows output from one servlet to be given to another servlet, either on the local computer or on a remote computer.

Connections to databases

Near-universal support on systems (for example, Windows, Linux, Solaris)

In order for Java servlets and other applications to function, however, you must first

install a Java Virtual Machine (JVM) on your system. You can obtain a JVM from various vendors.

Content Management System (CMS)
A Content Management System (CMS) is a server or series of servers that allows you to

easily create, store and track all documents and information produced by an organization. A CMS resides on a server, and is designed to accept and organize content submissions. Large and small organizations alike use CMS systems to help ensure that

employees can create and access information efficiently, and reduce duplication of effort

and time wasted searching for content.

Benefits of using a CMS include:

Centralized management of content — All information and work is stored and organized in one place, where it can be administered properly.

The ability to reuse content — Once content is properly stored, that content can be reused in numerous ways to benefit the company.

Increased collaboration — A CMS can capture institutional knowledge about products and procedures, and make it readily available.

Role management

A CMS requires companies to determine roles for each user. Following are examples of

CMS roles:

Creators/owners/authors — users who are able to generate and modify content. However, they often can work only on their own content, and not that of others.

Managers — users who have been given all permissions over those who they supervise. Managers can alter or discard content, even if they do not own the content. Managers can define users on the system, as well as change content

ownership, and create new projects and directories. Also called "supervisors" in some

CMS applications.

Editors — users who have the ability to make content changes.

Reviewers — users who have the ability to leave comments or make suggestions about content changes, but are not allowed to make any changes.

Publishers — users who have the ability to view content, but also to create comparison, or differential, documents to determine what has occurred over time.

Viewers — users who can view content, but not alter it in any way. Depending upon the capabilities of the CMS, viewers may or may not be able to print or download content.

Administrators — users who have full control over the system.

Permission management

Permissions can be managed in various ways, including:

Directory services servers (Microsoft Active Directory, Open LDAP, Novell Directory

Services).

Public Key Infrastructure (PKI).

Content publication
A CMS is responsible for ensuring that content can be published to users based on the

permissions that have been established.

Content editing
A sophisticated CMS provides editing tools that make it easy for individuals to edit content.

Version control
A CMS can manage multiple submissions of the same document. Whenever two or more users edit the same document, a race condition is said to exist. This condition can cause important information and changes to be lost. If two or more users attempt to edit a file,

the CMS will either lock out all but one user, or otherwise manage the submissions so

that both sets of changes are integrated in alternative documents. As a result, all user

submissions are saved. A CMS thus helps reduce the duplication of effort.

Another element of version control is the ability for the CMS to create backup copies of

documents that have been edited. Users can refer to these copies and determine what

changes have been made. A CMS can also create a special document called a differential

document. This document allows users to trace the changes that have been made to the original document over time.

The practice of version control is also called revision control or versioning

Indexing and searching

A CMS implementation makes a site easily searchable. Many companies will implement a

CMS for this reason alone. Sometimes, searches are conducted through third-party

services such as Google. However, most CMS servers include native search capability.

Caching and replication

A CMS is capable of creating copies of content and distributing them to additional

servers. This strategy of load balancing ensures quick access to documents because

information is distributed among multiple CMS servers. Caching content is usually done

internally by the CMS, and helps ensure that often-used content is readily available.

Simplified backup

Because a CMS stores information centrally, this information can be readily backed up. Backup ensures that

content is still available despite a catastrophic event, such as a hard disk failure, a power

supply failure, or an incident involving severe weather or vandalism.

Backup options include:

1. Creating a tape backup.

2. Sending files to a third-party for backup.

Syndication

The practice of syndication involves making content available via an RSS (Really Simple Syndication) or Atom feed, or via e-mail.

CMS as a workflow management tool

As you can see, a CMS is more than a place to store files. It is a workflow management tool that helps managers and executives ensure that users properly submit and manage content. As long as the company has properly defined roles for users, and the CMS has been properly configured to reflect these roles, the CMS server becomes a central tool that ensures content is updated properly and remains available to the correct individuals. It is also common for companies to use a CMS to help manage the submission and

editing of Web site pages and content.

Requirements analysis

Implementing a CMS properly requires more than just installing a server and populating it with content. You will need to conduct a high-level analysis of your company's needs. This analysis involves determining server requirements, as well as

your company's structure.

As you determine server requirements, consider the following:

Number of users

Projected server load

Storage capacity

You will need to configure the CMS to support and enforce the job roles you have defined

in your company. Consider the following:

Mapping department job roles and functions to CMS roles - Work closely with department managers to determine exact job functions as you map the

CMS roles to the actual job roles in your company. Create sample CMS roles, and ask the managers and their workers to confirm that the roles you have defined accurately reflect the job roles.

Existing resources - You will likely need to connect your CMS to other company resources, including Web servers, databases, media servers, and file and print servers. Gather these requirements and create a network map to ensure that the

implementation will go smoothly.

Workflow management

One of the functions of a CMS is to provide notifications regarding document ownership and the state of a particular project. With one glance, an individual can review the

progress of a particular document from creation through editing and publishing. Workflow management also involves the ability for managers to approve key activities and essential steps as a project moves towards completion. A CMS has the ability to track these approvals to help guide the project along, and to help managers conduct a forensic analysis of past projects. A forensic analysis is a process in which managers investigate a past project to determine where the project succeeded, and what could have been done to overcome any challenges that occurred.

Content acquisition

When working with a CMS, make sure that you consider the following issues:

Ease of submission

Time to create content

A properly configured and managed CMS is the best way to capture the institutional

knowledge of a particular organization. This is primarily because a CMS is designed to

facilitate group participation and document editing. As you acquire content, make sure

that you encourage the use of the following:

Peer-based editing - Everyone should be encouraged to make constructive changes. The point of a CMS is to capture the wisdom of the entire organization, not just one individual or group of individuals. Collaboration between multiple workers on a

document is critical to success.

Wikis - A wiki enables individuals to freely communicate in a relatively open

environment. Consider using a wiki to help create or modify a document, rather than focusing on trying to complete and perfect it with each edit.

Standard tagging

The practice of marking content is often called "tagging." Tagging content ensures that the content is published in an orderly fashion. Specifically, tagging ensures that new content:

Does not conflict with separate submissions from other individuals. If potential

conflicts occur, multiple submissions will be logged and stored.

Is properly tracked so that previous versions can be used and compared with current

content versions.

Is logged.

Taxonomic and social tagging

Tagging involves using a technology to identify and rank information as being more or

less useful. A CMS most often uses Extensible Markup Language (XML) to conduct

tagging. Two types of tagging exist:

Standard — A specified individual or group of individuals, considered expert(s) in the related field, determines content relevance and accuracy.

The strength of this form of

tagging is that experts can apply their expertise to the process.

Weaknesses: Individuals can become overwhelmed and biased. Traditional tagging is often referred to as applying a taxonomy, or weighting content.

Social — All users, or a defined group of users (non-experts), have the ability to weigh in on content. Social tagging is often referred to as applying a folksonomy, or crowdsourcing.

Strength: It is much easier to

determine what the majority of end users need.

Weakness: Particular documents or tasks that are unpopular still need to be used and read.

Template creation and management

A CMS often uses templates to standardize the document-creation process and ensure a consistent look and feel for all content created.

Templates ensure:

A consistent look and feel for all documents. This includes standard branding.

That all parties receive standard information and instructions for each document

being edited.

Localization

Localization is the practice of either translating documents to another language, or

otherwise altering wording and other content to better suit a particular culture or system

of values. Localization concerns include:

On the fly localization — the ability to localize a Web page to various languages through an end-user request.

Character sets — Standard character sets can include UTF-8 (Unicode), the Universal Character Set (ISO/IEC 10646) and various language-specific character sets.

Language direction — Some languages are read right to left (RTL), whereas others

are read left to right (LTR).

Personalization and portals

Personalization involves customizing content on the fly for a particular user or type of

user. Using various technologies, it is possible to personalize a user's CMS experience. Technologies can include:

Role-based customization — As a user logs in, interface elements are made available or omitted depending upon the user's role and permissions.

User-set preferences — A user is often allowed to set preferences, default directories

and other settings based on permissions.

It is possible to enforce custom environments and record preferences using cookies and

login scripts. When content has been sufficiently personalized, the CMS is said to have turned a Web site into a portal (as opposed to a static Web site).

In many cases, an administrator may decide to convert a personalized page created by a

CMS into a static page that always remains available. Such pages are said to be "baked"

because they are now always static. The advantage of a baked page is that the CMS does not have to constantly generate this page from scratch at every user request. In many cases, a baked page is created to reduce the CMS workload. When a CMS creates a new page dynamically, that page is said to be "fried."

CMS and the content life cycle

A simplified life cycle includes the following stages:

Creation — the development of all content that goes into the CMS. Includes the submission of content, as well as all peer-based evaluation and editing work. Also called acquisition.

Management — The CMS and administrators organize and prioritize content based on permissions and job roles. Also involves workflow management steps and reporting, as well as placing content into individual repositories and databases.

Delivery — includes publishing content to Web servers, e-commerce servers, wikis and syndication services. Content is published according to predetermined rules that

specify which users are allowed to read various types of content.

Evaluation — determines how existing content needs to be changed or if it needs to

be discarded. Content deletion is often referred to as content destruction.

Re-development — Existing content is altered and then reintroduced to the CMS.

CMS security concerns

You can solve security problems by making sure that automatic login features are not enabled, and by educating users to make sure they check the profile they are using whenever they log in to the CMS.

Web CMS

Perhaps the most common type of CMS is Web CMS, which is designed specifically to

manage the submission of content onto one or more Web servers. Another term for Web CMS is portal. A Web CMS has the following responsibilities and features:

Tools that allow occasional users of HTML and other languages to create relatively

sophisticated Web pages

Workflow management capabilities

The ability to cache and compare previously created pages

Content syndication

An enterprise CMS serves more than just the organization's Web servers. Additional

systems that the CMS can manage include:

Human resources.

Shipping and delivery.

Payment and invoice systems.

Customer relations.

Sales management.

Server Command Line TOOLS

Microsoft's version of a command line interface or CLI.
Command Prompt

Running the command prompt as an administrator is also known as running it in _____.
Elevated Mode

This displays the help file for ipconfig.
ipconfig /?

Type the command _____ to retrieve an IP address and other IP configurations.
ipconfig /renew

Used to test the existence of other hosts on the network.
Ping

To find out the host name of a computer, type either the command _____ or the command _____.
Hostname / Ipconfig

This command option sends pings endlessly to a destination IP address.
Ping -t [IP address]

The ping -t command can only be stopped by pressing this on the keyboard.

Ctrl + C

This displays TCP and UDP connections.

netstat -a (command)

This displays TCP and UDP connections in numeric format.

netstat -an (command)

This displays Ethernet statistics such as the number of packets and bytes sent and received.

netstat -e (command)

This displays the route table.

netstat -r (command)

This displays statistics per protocol, such as TCP, UDP, ICMP, IP, etc...

netstat -s (command)

This displays NetBIOS over TCP/IP statistics for local and remote computers.

nbtstat (command)

This displays NetBIOS name resolution statistics.

nbtstat -r (command)

This purges the contents of the NetBIOS name cache table.
nbtstat -R (command)

This releases and refreshes NetBIOS names.
netstat -RR (command)

This displays NetBIOS sessions and attempts to convert the remote IP addresses to names.
nbtstat -s (command)

This displays NetBIOS sessions and attempts to convert the remote IP addresses to names and the remote computers are listed by IP address.
nbtstat -S (command)

Shows paths to a destination on another network.
tracert (command)

Shows paths to a destination on another network numerically.
tracert -d (command)

Shows paths to a destination on another network as well as the degree of packet loss.
pathping (command)

Displays information about DNS names and their corresponding IP addresses, and it can be used to diagnose DNS servers.
nslookup (command)

Used to take control of a remote computer.
telnet (command)

A built-in command-line scripting utility that enables you to display and modify the network configurations of the local computer.
netsh (command)

Enables you to display and make changes to the local IP routing table of the computer.
route (command)

A distance vector protocol that uses algorithms to decipher which route to send data packets.
Routing Information Protocol (RIP)

A link-state protocol that monitors the network for routers that have a change in their link-state, meaning whether they were turned off/on/restarted.
Open Shortest Path First (OSPF)

Allows you to configure various networking options such as services.
net (command)

Shows the computers on your immediate network, whether they operate as a workgroup or a domain.
net view (command)

This can be used when mapping drives and connecting to computers for other reasons.
Universal Naming Convention

Used in the command prompt to connect to FTP servers.
FTP (command)

What command displays the IP address, subnet mask, and default gateway of the system you are currently on?
Ipconfig

What protocol does the ping command use to test network connectivity?
ICMP

What command do you use to clear the DNS cache on a local system?
Ipconfig /flushdns

What command do you use to test a system's IPv4 protocol stack?
Ping 127.0.0.1

What command do you use to display active TCP or UDP connections?
Netstat

Server Vocabulary

Active Directory (AD)

The directory service included with Windows Server 2003 that provides a single point of administration, authentication, and storage for user, group, and computer objects.

Forest

A collection of Active Directory trees that do not necessarily share a contiguous DNS naming convention but do share a common global catalog and schema.

Forest root domain

The first domain created with the Active Directory structure.

Lightweight Directory Access Protocol

(LDAP)

An access protocol that defines how users can access or update directory service objects.

Member Server

A windows Server 2003 system that has a computer account in a domain, but is not configured as a domain controller.

Organizational Unit

(OU)

An Active Directory logical container used to organize objects within a single domain. Objects such as users, groups, computers, and other OUs can be stored within a OU container.

Site
A combination of one or more Internet Protocol subnets connected by a high-speed link.

Software Update Services

(SUS)
Microsoft software that allows security patches and updates to be deployed from a centralized server.

Driver signing
A digital signature that Microsoft incorporates into driver and system files as a way to verify the files and to ensure that they are not inappropriately overwritten.

File Signature Verification
A utility used to identify unsigned system and driver files, that provides information such as the file name, location, modification date, and version number.

Hardware Profile
A set of instructions telling the operating system which devices to start and drivers to load when a computer starts.

Uninterpretable Power Supply

(UPS)

A device built into electrical equipment or a separate device that provides immediate battery power to equipment during a power failure or brownout.

Windows Server Catalog

The main listing of hardware devices that have been certified to function with Windows Server 2003, and officially carry the "Designed for Windows Server 2003" logo

Active Directory Users and Catalog

An Active Directory MMC tool that allows you to create various objects such as OUs, user accounts, groups, computers, and contacts.

Group Policy

Enables the centralized management of user desktop setting, desktop and domain security, and the deployment and management of software throughout your network.

Kerberos v5

The primary authentication protocol used in Active Directory domain environments.

Roaming profile

A user profile stored on a centralized server that allows a user access a network.

User Account

An object that is stored in Active Directory that represents all of the information that defines a physical user who has access permissions to the network.

User Account Template

An special user account configured with settings that are copied in order to simplify the creation of user accounts with common settings.

Authentication

The process by which a user's identity is validated, which is subsequently used to grant or deny access to network resources.

NT LAN Manager

(NTLAM)

The challenge-response protocol that is used for authentication purposes with operating systems running Windows NT or earlier.

Object

A collection of attributes that represents items within Active Directory such as users, groups, computers, and printers.

Security Accounts Manager

(SAM)

The local security and accounts database on a Windows 2003 standalone and member server.

Paging File

Disk space, in the form of a file (pagefiles.sys), for use when memory requirements exceed the available RAM.

Virtual Memory

Disk storage used to extend the capacity of the physical RAM installed in a computer.

Distribution Group

A group that is only used for an e-mail distribution list.

Domain Local Group

A group that only be assigned permissions to a resource available in the domain in which it is created. However, group membership can come from any domain within the forest. Created on domain controllers within the domain.

Global groups

A group that is mainly sued for organizing other objects into administrative units. A global group can be assigned permissions to any resource in any domain within the forest. The main limitation is that it can only contain members of the same domain in which it is created.

Security group

A group that can be used to define permissions on a resource object.

Universal Group

A group that can be assigned permissions to any resource in any domain within the forest. These groups can consist of any user or group object except for local groups.

Windows 2000 Mixed Mode

The default domain function level for a Windows Server 2000 Active Directory Domain. Supports Windows NT Server 4.0, Windows 2000 Server, and Windows Server 2003 domain controllers.

Windows 2000 Native Mode

A domain Functional level that supports both Windows 2000 Server and Windows Server 2003 domain controllers.

Windows Server 2003 Mode
A domain functional level that supports Windows Server 2003 domain controllers only.

Access of Control Entry/ ACE
An entry in an object's discretionary access control list that grants permissions to a user or group. It is also an entry in an object's system access control list that specifies the security events to be audited for a user or group.

Administrative Shares
Hidden shared folders created for the purpose of allowing administrators to access the root partitions and other system folders remotely.

Computer Management Console
A predefined Microsoft Management Console application that allows administration of a variety of computer related tasks on the local computer or a remote computer.

Disk Management
The Windows Server 2003 utility used to manage disk partitions and volumes.

Shared Folder
A data resource container that has been made available over the network to authorize network clients.

NTFS Permissions
The permissions available on the Security tab on an NTFS file or folder.

Defragmenting

A process by which fragmented files are rearranged into contiguous areas of disk space, improving file access performance.

Extended Partition

A partition on a basic disk that is created from unpartitioned free disk space, and is not formatted with a file system. The space is allocated to logical drives.

Fault Tolerance

Techniques that employ hardware and software to provide assurance against equipment failures, computer service interruptions, and data loss.

Fragmented

A normal and gradual process in which files become divided into different areas of disk space in a volume, resulting in slower file access.

Mirrored Volume

A fault-tolerated disk strategy in which a volume on one dynamic disk has its contents mirrored to a second dynamic disk.

Mounted Drive

A partition or volume accessible via an empty folder on an existing NTFS partition. Often implemented to circumvent the need to assign the column or partition a drive letter.

Compression

An advanced attribute of the NTFS file system used to reduce the amount of space that files and folders occupy on a partition or volume.

Data Recovery Agent

A user account capable of gaining access to EFS-encrypted files encrypted by other users. In a domain environment, the domain Administrator account is the default data recover agent.

Disk Quotas
A Windows Server 2003 feature that is used as means of monitoring and controlling the amount of disk space available to users.

Domain Based DFS Model
A distributed resource model that uses Active Directory and is available only to servers and workstations that are members of a particular domain. This enables a deep root-based hierarchical arrangement of shared folders that is published in Active Directory; allows replication for fault tolerance and load balancing.

Standalone DFS Model
A distributed resource model in which there is no Active Directory implemented to help manage the shared folders. This model provides only a single or flat level share.

Print Driver
Files that contain information that Windows 2003 uses to convert raw print commands to a language that the printer understands.

Graphics Device Interface

GDI
An interface on a Windows network print client that works with a local software application, such as Microsoft Word, and a local printer driver to format a file to be sent to a local or network print server.

Printer Permissions

Security permissions that allow an administrator to control access to printer resources, in a manner similar to NTFS permissions.

Printer Properties

Configuring multiple logical prints to print to the same print device. One printer is then configured to print before other printers by adjusting the priority setting from 1 (lowest level) to 99 (highest level)

RAW

A data type often used for printing MS-DOS, Windows 3.x, and UNIX print files.

Default Domain Policy

The name of the GPO that is linked to the domain container in the Active Directory; used primarily for configuration of domain-wide password policies.

Folder Redirection

A group policy feature that enables you to redirect the contents of the Application Data, Desktop, My Documents, My Pictures, and Start Menu folders from a user's profile to a network domain.

Globally Unique Identifier

(GUID)

A unique 128-bit number assigned to the object when it is created.

Group Policy

Enables the centralized management of user desktop settings, desktop and domain security, and the deployment and management of software throughout your network.

Group Policy Object

(GPO)
An Active Directory object that is configured to apply Group Policy and linked to wither the site, domain, or OU level.

Microsoft Windows Installer Package
A file that contains all of the information needed to install an application in a variety of configurations.

ZAP File
A text file that can be used by Group Policy to deploy an application; it has a number of limitations compared to a MSI file.

Delegation of Control Wizard
The wizard available in Active Directory Users and Computers to simplify the delegation of administrative authority.

Management Saved Console

MSC
The extension associated with a saved MMC file.

Terminal Services
A Windows Server 2003 feature that allows users to connect to a Windows Server 2003 system and interact with applications as if sitting at the server console.

Windows Update
The Windows feature that allows operating systems to download service packs, patches, and hot fixes from Microsoft in an automated fashion rather than by manual downloads.

Application log

Where applications that are written to Microsoft standards record event information. The application developer determines the type of information an application writes to the log file.

Performance console

A pre-defined MMC that includes both the System Monitor and Performance logs and Alert tools.

Performance Logs and Alerts

A tool included with Windows Server 2003 that enables you to create counter logs, trace logs, and configure alerts.

System Monitor

A tool that allows you to gather and view real-time performance statistics of a local or network computer.

Task Manager

A tool used to view the processes and applications currently running on the system. Also provides basic resource usage statistics.

Trace Logs

Where data provider collects performance data when an even occurs

Performance counters

Data items associated with a particular object used to measure a certain aspect of system performance.

GPRESULT

The utility that can be used to discover Group Policy-related problems and to illustrate which GPOs were applied to a user or computer. It also lists all group memberships of the user or computer being analyzed.

Resultant Set of Policy

(RSoP)

A graphical utility included with Windows Server 2003 that enables you to review the aggregated Group Policy setting that apply to a domain user or computer.

Automated System Recovery

ASR

A new Windows 2003 feature that allows an administrator to restore server configuration setting in the event that a system cannot be repaired using other methods such as safe mode or last knows good configuration.

Backup Utility

The tool included with Windows Server 2003 that enables administrators to back up and restore data system configurations in case of a hardware or software failure.

Normal Backup

A backup type that backs up all selected files and folders, and clears the archive attribute on these files and folders.

Incremental Backup

A method of baking up selected files that have been created or modified since the last normal or incremental backup and clears the archive attribute associated with the files.

Deferential Backup

A method of backing up selected files that have been created or modified since the last full backup but does not clear the archive attribute.

Daily Backup

A method of backing up only the selected files that have been created or modified on the day that the backup is being performed. They are not marked as being backed up.

Safe Mode

An advanced boot option that allows a Windows Server 2003 system to be booted with minimal services or drivers loaded, typically used for troubleshooting or diagnostic purposes.

Show Copies of Shared Files

A new feature in Windows Server 2003 that can be enabled on a volume-by-volume basis to allow a user to view or recover previous versions of files stored in shared folders.

System State

A group of critical operating system files and components that can be backed up as a single group on a Windows Server 2003 system. System State data always includes the Registry, COM+ Registration Data, boot files and system files.

Anonymous Access

Allows users to access a Web site without having to provide a user name and password.

Authentication

Refers to determining whether a user has a valid user account with proper permissions to access a resource such as a shared folder or Web site.

Bandwidth Throttling
Allows you to limit the network bandwidth that is available for Web and FTP connections to the server.

Digest Authentication
Prompts users for a user name and password to be able to access a Web Resource. The user name and password are hashed to prevent hackers from obtaining the information.

Internet Information Services
A Windows Server 2003 component that provides Web-related services to an organization.

Metabase
The database that IIS 6.0 stores its configuration setting in.

SO Do you know?

If a Raid 5 array with 3 drives has one drive showing RED, what do you do?
Replace the drive

During the install of a printer driver, the error states that it didn't pass the Windows logo testing, what should you do?

Use a Microsoft Certified Driver

When creating a new data retention policy, should you consider "applicable laws, rules and regulations first?

yes

Define Blade Server

A chassis types that uses space for performance most effectively

An outcome that would result in firmware update that fails during a power outage or interruption?

Damage of the hardware

Define Server virtualization

a single physical server to host multiple logical servers to

effectively utilize hardware resources

Define HBA

A card installed into a server for SAN connectivity via Fiber

ISA Component

16 Bit Bus

A server needs maximum face, no fault tolerance and 4 drives, use what Raid?

RAID 0

What is Raid 3?

Uses Fault Tolerance writing parity to 1 drive

data backups
Are used for Disaster Recovery

Data Archives
Used for Record Purposes, kept for indefinite amount of time

What happens when a server has a BOOT password enabled?
a password is needed in order for the

server to begin the start up process

For Banks and Hospitals, what must you follow to dispose of their equipment?
Local Rules, Laws and Regulations

Minimum Drives in a RAID 10?
4

What role provides a Common Time to all PC's?
NTP

What storage device has the most individual drive storage available?
SATA

When triaging an issue, what is the first step to resolve?
Identify the problem

If a Computer's account is removed from AD, what error results when logging in on that PC?

System cannot log you on to the domain because the system's computer account in its primary domain is missing or the password on that account is incorrect

If the page file is out of space, what results?

Slow performance, error message "System out of Virtual Memory"

If you get "Access Denied" when trying to end a task in Task Manager, what do you use?

Kill Utility

If the Server has two drives and the C Drive is running out of space, what is an action to take if possible?

Move the Page file to the other drive

What log do you look at to see "Unauthorized logins"?

Security Log

For RAID 1, if the drives are setup as basic, what cannot happen?

You cannot use the Mirroring Option

Virtualization is improved in performance by what upgrade?

Memory

Define NAS

Drives presented as storage to multiple servers in an existing network.

Current Physical Layouts should be documented where?
Rack Diagrams

Define Ducts and Baffles
Channels air flow through a Server

What protocol is used to test if a host is reachable from another using Echos?
ICMP

What would cause all of the drives in a RAID 5 array to go offline?
A Bad SCSI Backplane

What backup types reset the archive bit?
GFS, Full and Incremental

Define DFS
Allows replication between servers (Microsoft)

What does an application exception do?
Allows internet software through the server firewall

Best RAID for fault tolerance?
RAID 10

What is the main requirement for distance involving a "Hot site"?
avoiding a regional disaster

Define Performance Monitor
Use to get a Server Baseline

Define Shadow Copies
Recover Deleted files on file shares

A server using RAID 5 has 5 disks with 100Gigs, how much disk space will be available for use?
400gb (1 drive is used as a spare. 500gb total - 100gb spare = 400gb)

What speed does the L3 Cache run?
The speed of the system bus.

Define ACL
restricts traffic from a host to a network

What is a difference from SATA and PATA?
SATA does not use jumpers

Main advantage of using a KVM?
Saves physical space in Server Racks

What failure is most likely causing the ability to eject a tape from a tape drive?
Drive Failure

New users are getting IP addresses that begin with 169. What should you check?
DHCP Server

What can be used to specify a set of FQDN to IP Mappings but not be seen by other servers?
Host File

Minimum drives for Raid 50?
6

Two methods to remotely have access to the Server Console?
VNC and Remote Desktop

How many VRM's are required for QUAD Xeon CPU's?
4

What do you use to see the number of network connections a server is making?
Netstat

Define Raid 3
stripes data at the bit level and uses a dedicated disk for parity

What RAIDs stripes data at the block level and does not have a dedicated disk for parity?
0 and 5

What hard drive bus is the fastest?
SAS

Define Multicore
Multiple cores on a single die

How do you ensure that a server is up-to-date with all updates as soon as they are released?
Configure Automatic updates to install automatically.

Telnet uses which port?
23

For best Performance with 4 hard drives, which RAID do you use?
0

Raid for two drives and a need for fault tolerance?
1

Define Hot Spare
drive assigned to an array that will automatically be used to rebuild a failed array drive

What port needs to be open for (RDP)Remote desktop connections?
3389

What would you use to have a network printer automatically installed when a user logs on?
Login Script

What server type stores users' home directory folders?
Directory Services

For Gigabit Ethernet Speeds use what cable?
CAT6

When disposing Data which is considered first?
Local legal requirements

What can you use to install an OS without a boot disc?
PXE

A server is not showing new memory that was just installed?
Reseat the memory.

Fastest way to deploy multiple servers with a new OS in a Virtual Environment?
Use a server template and build all servers from this template

Define a Mantrap
Security measure requires people entering or leaving the datacenter to go through an extra secure area. Once entering the area people must present two forms of authentication to leave.

If you need to have a database with low seek time, what should you use?
a Single Solid State Drive

In a Shared Datacenter, what is a best practice to prevent theft of information?
Locked Service Rack Doors

Consult the HCL for what info when installing Memory?
Memory and Speed Compatibility

Define Software Firewall
Decreases the overall attack surface of the servers by decreasing the number of open network ports on each server

Define SLA
Level of service including time limits for service, repair and replacement

What is always the first step to follow when reacting to a fire in the datacenter?
Evacuate all personnel

Fact: Data Backups
Contain data that is still on the server

Temperate Range recommended for a datacenter?
64F to 77F (18c to 25c)

Most Secure way to dispose of rewritable DVD media with data?

Shredding

What command to use on a Windows server to reboot remotely without console access?
shutdown

Fact about Upgrading BIOS
Follow Manufacturer instructions

Fact: Server to Server Replication
Provides a greater overall fault tolerance over disk to disk

Backup and Storage Devices:
NAS, SAN and Tape Libraries

Define Load Balancing
Connecting to a server in a server farm with the lowest CPU Utilization

Where do you change the BOOT order of devices?
BIOS

FACT: Non-ECC Memory
NON-ECC Memory is faster than ECC Memory

Fact: HCL Devices
Meets vendor standards

Computers with 32 bit CPU's can only go up to how much memory?
4gb

What do you need on a server to do "Teaming"?
Two NICs

What automatically assigns IP addresses?
DHCP

Fact: Service Tag
is used to look up the warranty information on the vendor's website.

Two big factors for a datacenter UPS:
Estimated Run time and Max Load

Fact: Caching Name Server
Authoritative and Recursive

After fixing a software issue that has been verified working, what should you do?
Update the baseline and document the process

When adding a drive to mirror the main OS drive you receive an error "Operating System not found". What is wrong?
The drive boot order is wrong.

Fact Sysprep
Must be done on a Windows server being used as a template

Where would you make the change if you wanted to block port 6000 except for 1 server?
Software Firewall Settings

What RAID to implement if you add 1 drive to a server that has one drive for OS and one for data and you don't want to lost anything?
Raid 1

Fact Redundant Power Sources:
You must have Multiple UPS and Redundant Power Supplies

Biggest RAID 0 advantage?
Speed

With more than 10 drives and the need for speed and redundancy, which Raid?
50

Fact: Online/Double Conversion UPS
used for equipment that is sensitive to power fluctuations

What should be checked first in a datacenter after finding a panel open on a server?
Datacenter Access log

Define DNS
allows a server to translate fully qualified domain names into IP addresses

Server Installation Order:

Install Server

Create Baseline

Label Server

Store Documentation

Update Network Diagram

Update Assets database

Biometric lock

Most secure for datacenters

Tool to use to determine if an ISP is failing?

Tracert

Fact: 2U

equals 3.5 in (8.89 cm)

Fact: Enterprise Class UNIX servers support the use of:

RISC Processing

HBA is used to connect:

Fiber Channel SAN

Minimum Subnet mask for 800 hosts?

255.255.252.0

Fact: Hardware RAID Controller
Minimizes the performance impact of Parity Overhead in Raid 5

Fact: iSCSI
transmit block level storage over Ethernet

Fact: Fiber Channel
uses a switching fabric to connect storage LUNs to hosts

If the humidity is too low in the Datacenter, what could happen?
A Risk of shocks

For a Virtualized machine what would be the fastest way to restore back to a pre-patched state if patching failed?
Snapshot

What Class is a fire suppression system?
C

Fact: Multimeter
Used to check voltage on a Power Supply

What is ROUTE used for on a Linux/Unix server?
used to set the default gateway on the server

In a RAID configuration, what tool is used to set partitions?

diskpart

Best backup media for Router Configuration files?
Flash drive

What should be done before installing Patches in a Production environment?
Test the patches in a Test Environment

Define hypervisor
Manages Virtual Machines

If a User's Account is locked, they:
cannot access Network Resources

Best way to expand Storage size in a flexible manner?
NAS (Network Attached Storage)

FACT: Hot Site
Disaster Recovery site with high uptime requirements and will lose money if there is any downtime.

Fact: hardware-based RAID controller
Accessible thru BIOS, Retains Data in the event of a power outage and accessible in the OS via System Utility

Fact: battery backed write cache
Prevent data loss on a RAID Array in the event of a power failure

HOT Swappable technologies?
SCSI and SAS

Fact: Cloning
Virtual Technology that can save time during provisioning

Disk Quotas are used for?
Implementing Storage Space Requirements per user

Minimum Virtual Memory Setting for a Computer?
1.5 times the amount of physical memory

What is needed to use Windows Software Update Services (WSUS)?
IIS

What is a FATHER backup?
Weekly scheduled backup

What should you use to remove dust from a Server?
Compressed Air

Warranty Expiration date should be stored?
in the Assets Management Database

If a server has a second cooling system in case of failure, it has:
Redundant Cooling

Fact: Serial Card
Used as inputs for external Measuring devices

How to clear an error on a user's PC trying to access a shared folder. The message states "error message that multiple connections to the same resource are not allowed".
Net use with the /delete parameter

Fact: Blade Server
Better Rack Space utilization than a typical server.

First thing to check if a new UPS starts beeping?
Make sure the Power Cable is plugged in.

Why should you avoid cooling a datacenter too quickly after a power outage?
Condensation will form causing an electrical risk.

Best Reason to perform Server Updates?
addresses Driver and Security issues.

At first report of a server performing poorly, what should you check?
Server baseline

Fact: Two factors in updating the firmware on a video card?
Video Chipset and Server Manufacturers

Best way to avoid downtime on a servers that could have possible hard drive downtime?
Purchase servers with hot swappable drives configured in a RAID

Which "ping option" would you use to convert numerical addresses to host names?
"-a"

Fact: SAS
Best data bandwidth when installing multiple external hard drives on a server

Fact: Network Adapter Teaming
Speed up web traffic on a single slow internet response server

3 Fault Tolerance Items:
Second Nic, Redundant Power Source and Uninterruptible Power Supply.

Fact: SCSI
required termination

Fact: Memory Modules
are susceptible to ESD

Max speed for iSCSI?
Equal to the speed of the link

Fact: SNMP Thresholds
Adjust if receiving many alerts for CPU Utilization

iSCSI
Defines the rules and processes used to transmit and receive block storage applications over TCP/IP

Fact: Securing Fiber Cables
Use only Velcro Cable Straps (others can damage the cable)

PC100 or PC133 memory is also known as:
SDRAM

PC2100 Memory is known as:
DDR

PC3-8500 Memory is known as:
DDR3

Socket 478 supports what CPU?
Pentium 4

A user states they are getting an error message with Port 23 involved. What is being used?
Telnet

FACT: WSUS
Used for Windows OS Updates

FACT: CAT6
4 Wire Pairs

Which RAID has the best performance and still have redundancy?
Raid 5

If an INTERNAL ZONE was deleted, the users can access External Websites but not?
Internal Sites

Critical Businesses that need file restoration in less than 4 hours should use:
SAN Replication

FACT: SAN
attaches to a server either through a fiber channel connection or is

presented to the server via iSCSI?

A server needs what to attach to a Fiber based SAN?
HBA (Host Bus Adapter)

FACT: Most Important Concern regarding Server Location:
Inadequate Air Flow

Define Multicore
allows a single physical processor to do the work of multiple processors

Which Raid combines Mirroring and Striping?
10

FACT: NAS
can slow down network traffic and uses TCP/IP

FACT: Blu-Ray
Greatest Storage Capacity

Raid with the Best Read and Write Performance
0

Memory utilization by the print spooler process is constantly climbing, what would cause this?
Memory Leak in the print driver.

Fact: Hardware RAID
performs faster than Software RAID

When Creating a data backup plan, the most important factor is:
Laws and Regulations of the Data

Most likely cause a server is overheating?
Dust

What backup strategy is the most time efficient for backing up data?
Incremental

Acronyms

*nix
Unix/Linux/Solaris/OS X/BSD

AD
Active Directory

AGP
Advanced Graphics Port

AMD-V
AMD Virtualization

BIOS
Basic Input/Output System

BSOD
Blue Screen of Death

CPU
Central Processing Unit

CRU
Customer Replaceable Unit

DC
Domain Controller

DHCP
Dynamic Host Control Protocol

DMZ
Demilitarized Zone

DNS
Domain Name Service

DSRM
Directory Services Restore Mode

EISA
Extended Industry Standard Architecture

FAT
File Allocation Table

FRU
Field Replaceable Unit

FTP
File Transfer Protocol

HBA
Host Bus Adapter
HCL
Hardware Compatibility List
HID
Human Interface Device
HTTP
Hyper Text Transport Protocol
HTTPS
Secure Hyper Text Transport Protocol
IMAP4
Internet Mail Access Protocol
ISA
Industry Standard Architecture
iSCSI
Internetworking Small Computer Serial Interface
JBOD
Just a bunch of disks
LAN
Local Area Network
LDAP
Lightweight Directory Access Protocol
LKGC
Last Known Good Configuration
LUN
Logical Unit Number
NOS
Network Operating System
NTFS
New Technology File System
NTP
Network Time Protocol
NX
No Execute
OS
Operating System
OSPF

Open Shortest Path First
PCI
Peripheral Component Interconnect
POP3
Post Office Protocol
RAID
Redundant Array of Inexpensive/Integrated Disks/Drives
RAM
Random Access Memory
SAS
Serial Attached SCSI
SATA
Serial ATA
SCSI
Small Computer Serial Interface
SLA
Service Level Agreement
SMTP
Simple Mail Transport Protocol
SNMP
Simple Network Management Protocol
TCP/IP
Transmission Control Protocol / Internet Protocol
USB
Universal Serial Bus
VLAN
Virtual Local Area Network
VM
Virtual Machine
VMFS
VMWare File System
VoIP
Voice over IP
VPN
Virtual Private Network
VT
Virtualization Technology

WBEM
Web-based Enterprise Management
WMI
Windows Management Instrumentation
WORM
Write Once Read Many
XD
Execute Disable

Check out our other Study Blast Books at http://www.studyblastbooks.com or find them on Http://www.amazon.com.

Some of our other titles:

Study Blast ITIL Foundations

Study Blast ITIL Managing Across the Life Cycle

Study Blast ITIL Service Operations

Study Blast ITIL Service Design

Study Blast ITIL Service Strategy

Study Blast ITIL Continual Service Improvement

Microsoft, Cisco, CIW, CompTIA, and others.

Coming soon on Kindle, iBooks, Nook, Sony and more.

10905690R00126

Printed in Great Britain
by Amazon.co.uk, Ltd.,
Marston Gate.